D0954382

"*Some Girls, Some Hats and Hitler* does not minimize the horrors of war or the Holocaust, but through Kanter's delightful hopefulness and spare, riveting writing, it presents an unusual memoir of an era that must not be forgotten."

—*Shelf Awareness*

"From Paris to Vienna to London, Kanter creates a vibrant tapestry of her incredible odyssey through one of the darkest periods in contemporary history. Romance, passion, and peril create an authentically vivid backdrop for this intimate chronicle."

—*Booklist*

"This book is a remarkable, first-hand account of life during the time, and the importance that fashion played in the survival of Kanter and her loved ones."

—fashionpulsedaily.com

"In prose that cuts straight to the bone, *Some Girls, Some Hats and Hitler* tells the true story of Trudi's astonishing journey from Vienna to Prague to blitzed London seeking safety for her and Walter amid the horror engulfing Europe. . . . enchanting . . . In these pages she is alive—vivid, tenacious and absolutely unforgettable."

—bookreporter.com

"Trudi Kanter relates the emotional roller coaster she was on in attempting to get to England with her parents and the love of her life, Walter. The reader shares their terror and resultant cycles of inertia, hope and finally galvanization of emotional resources that Ms. Kanter, her family and friends all brought to bear."

—*Jewish Book World*

"In a rediscovered memoir, the charmed life of designer Trudi Kanter is split open as the Nazis claim Vienna and terror reigns. Every Holocaust story is worth remembering, and Trudi's is unique—she refuses to lose her vision of what the world should be at its very best: a place of red roses, Paris avenues, and above all else, true love."

—Alice Hoffman, author of *The Museum of Extraordinary Things* and *The Dovekeepers*

"Nothing undid beauty and romance like the onslaught of World War II. And yet in Trudi Kanter's elegant memoir *Some Girls, Some Hats and Hitler,* love and grace survive the horror in Western Europe. What an enchanting book. What a gem. I could not put it down."

—Jennifer Gilmore, author of *The Mothers*

"This Holocaust memoir is more a tale of love than a horror story of Nazi-occupied Europe. . . . the words and imagery flow beautifully."

—*Publishers Weekly*

"Distilled through the lens of a sartorial dignitary, *Some Girls, Some Hats and Hitler* offers an illuminating chronicle of narrow wartime escapes, calamity and ingenuity. What makes this account all the more revealing is its candor regarding the persistence of mortal tendencies amid even the most disastrous of situations. Sometimes there is vanity, sometimes jealousy and often, in the most unexpected of places, beauty of both the aesthetic and human varieties."

—Alicia Oltuski, author of *Precious Objects*

"A fascinating romance, a tribute to the love that beat Hitler."

—*Daily Post* (UK)

"A wonderful memoir of a young milliner in pre–World War II Vienna who flees to London with the man she loves when Hitler's tanks invade. Despite the tragic subject matter, this warm and vividly humorous autobiography is a must for anyone interested in fashion, history—and love."

—*Bella*

SOME GIRLS, SOME HATS and HITLER

A True Love Story

TRUDI KANTER

SCRIBNER

New York   London   Toronto   Sydney   New Delhi

This text, edited by Virago Press, is a version of the self-published edition of *Some Girls, Some Hats and Hitler,* which appeared in 1984. Very little is known of Trudi Kanter's life after Walter's death. Virago Press has been unable to trace the copyright holder in *Some Girls, Some Hats and Hitler,* and would be pleased to hear from anyone with any further information.

Scribner
A Division of Simon & Schuster, Inc.
1230 Avenue of the Americas
New York, NY 10020

First Scribner trade paperback edition January 2014

SCRIBNER and design are registered trademarks of The Gale Group, Inc.,
used under license by Simon & Schuster, Inc., the publisher of this work.

For information about special discounts for bulk purchases, please contact
Simon & Schuster Special Sales at 1-866-506-1949 or
business@simonandschuster.com.

The Simon & Schuster Speakers Bureau can bring authors to your
live event. For more information or to book an event contact the
Simon & Schuster Speakers Bureau at 1-866-248-3049 or
visit our website at www.simonspeakers.com.

Book design by Ellen R. Sasahara

Manufactured in the United States of America

1   3   5   7   9   10   8   6   4   2

Library of Congress Cataloging-in-Publication Data is available.

ISBN 978-1-4516-8830-6
ISBN 978-1-4767-0028-1 (pbk)
ISBN 978-1-4516-9659-2 (ebook)

Walter, my love. In memory.

Contents

Introduction

Linda Grant

When the Nazis marched into Austria in 1938, welcomed by cheering crowds, Trudi Kanter made an artistic decision in her millinery business. Just returned home to Vienna from a buying trip to Paris, she found that "the mob now had the upper hand . . . Worked up, ordered by their leaders to commit terrible crimes, they did as they were told." Trudi's new collection reflected the new reality: she decided she would use more veiling, to hide the sadness in women's eyes.

That fashion is more than surface, and that it says something about the times those who wear it live through, is an idea Trudi would have readily agreed with. She worked in the fripperies trade, but she understood how a feather or a piece of lace could raise the morale of depressed and frightened women, for she was dodging those terrifying crimes herself from day to day. Trudi Kanter was a witness to history, but she saw it from an unusual angle, that of an ambitious, romantic, sexy, half-Jewish business-woman in the fashion industry. From such an oblique viewpoint, we can observe how the lives of middle-class women went on or were interrupted by the tectonic plates of the twentieth century, and how some people survived through sheer chutzpah while others went under. For even in Nazi Vienna, she realized, women still looked in the mirror.

In the early 1980s, when she was approaching eighty herself, Trudi Kanter wrote a book, a memoir of her great love story: her marriage to Walter, the love of her life, and how this disciplined, wily woman got the two of them out of Austria to safety in London. It was published by a small press, went out of print, and was forgotten, which seems unjust, for Trudi was a natural writer; her prose fizzes with vitality, energy, humor, and a pinpoint recall of what she regards as beautiful.

Born Gertrude Sturmwind in 1905, the daughter of a Viennese jeweler, by her early thirties she had been married once, in a grand synagogue wedding, and was about to fall in love with Walter Ehrlich, a good-looking man who, after bumping into her on the street one lunchtime, invited her for lobster and champagne. Who was Walter? A successful businessman with matinee-idol looks, "thick, shiny hair, graying at the temples [and] olive skin." From the word go, Trudi was smitten. On her second date she wore a lilac chiffon dress with her hair up; on the third, he took her to dinner and she put on a white linen dress, white sandals, and carried an emerald green handbag. Walter wore a dark gray bespoke flannel suit, white brogues with black toes, and a white silk shirt.

But for all his charm, Walter had the self-preservation instincts of a dodo. On Trudi's return from Paris, her ears ringing with warnings that they must leave Austria at once while there was still time, Walter dug in his heels. He wanted time to reflect and consider, and refused to slink out of his country like a criminal. If he left, he told Trudi, it would be with head held high. Later that day, the Germans marched in and the borders were sealed.

Trudi and Walter were fashionable, trivial people. Yet Nazi Austria brought out the best in her: it was she who cajoled, begged, and charmed their way to safety in London, and brought out her elderly parents. None of Walter's family survived. London, just before the start of the war, seen through Trudi's eyes, is a drab, impoverished place; nothing like the elegance of Vienna or Paris is found in its prosaic streets. With sharp eyes and excellent recall she notices what everyone is wearing and what is fashionable ("brown, tan, gorse green . . . Nightdresses have changed from pale blue and pink cotton to red and blue floral flannel"), while she tries to find a job to keep her family afloat, eventually negotiating a business partnership for herself. Shockingly, both Walter and her father are interned as enemy aliens, and once again, it is Trudi who campaigns for their release.

Trudi was an only child and had no children. The Jewish Refugee Committee holds records of her arrival in London; she and Walter both became naturalized British citizens and changed their name from Ehrlich to Ellis. We know that after Walter's death in 1960 she married for a third time, and that her husband, who survived her, died intestate. Even her date of death is unknown, and no copyright holder for her book has as yet been identified. A letter to the *Jewish Chronicle* by the publishers of this edition produced no responses.

The mideighties was a time before the fashion for the memoir, and before publishers became interested in accounts of the Holocaust by ordinary individuals, so she had two strikes against her. There was, too, I think, an instinctive shrinking away from accounts of the war that did not treat it with the seriousness and solemnity of historians. Trudi must have seemed too shallow, too preoccupied with hats and men to be a sympathetic narrator of the life of the refugee. After all, the émigrés and exiles who flooded to England in the thirties, Sigmund Freud among them, were conductors, composers, poets, publishers, and cinematographers. Milliners were de trop. Her book went down into oblivion. Some readers believed it to be a novel.

And yet one hundred and seven years after her birth, Trudi Kanter seems now to be a heroine for the modern age, successful, independent, smart, and determined. Until the second half of the twentieth century, the fashion and beauty industries were two of the few regions of commerce where it was acceptable for women to play leading roles, to make their mark and be in control. The Parisian design houses were dominated by women (Chanel, Lanvin, Schiaparelli, Vionnet), and Helena Rubenstein, Elizabeth Arden, and Estee Lauder established global brands. It was because fashion was (and still is) regarded as inconsequential that women were permitted to dominate it, and to have the autonomy and decision-making that was closed off to them in other businesses. Trudi thrived because she had chosen a line of work in which she could exercise some power and which transcended national borders. The evidence that at the end of her life she was going to creative writing classes shows that she was unafraid to try something new.

Trudi was a survivor. Her book is also about the appetite for life, for clothes and hats and food and cocktails, sex and furnishings and good company and conversation. She knows that even in the bleak darkness, we feel, love, desire. She left no child (she and Walter tried, with no success); her hats are long lost, but her book is her legacy, discovered once again.

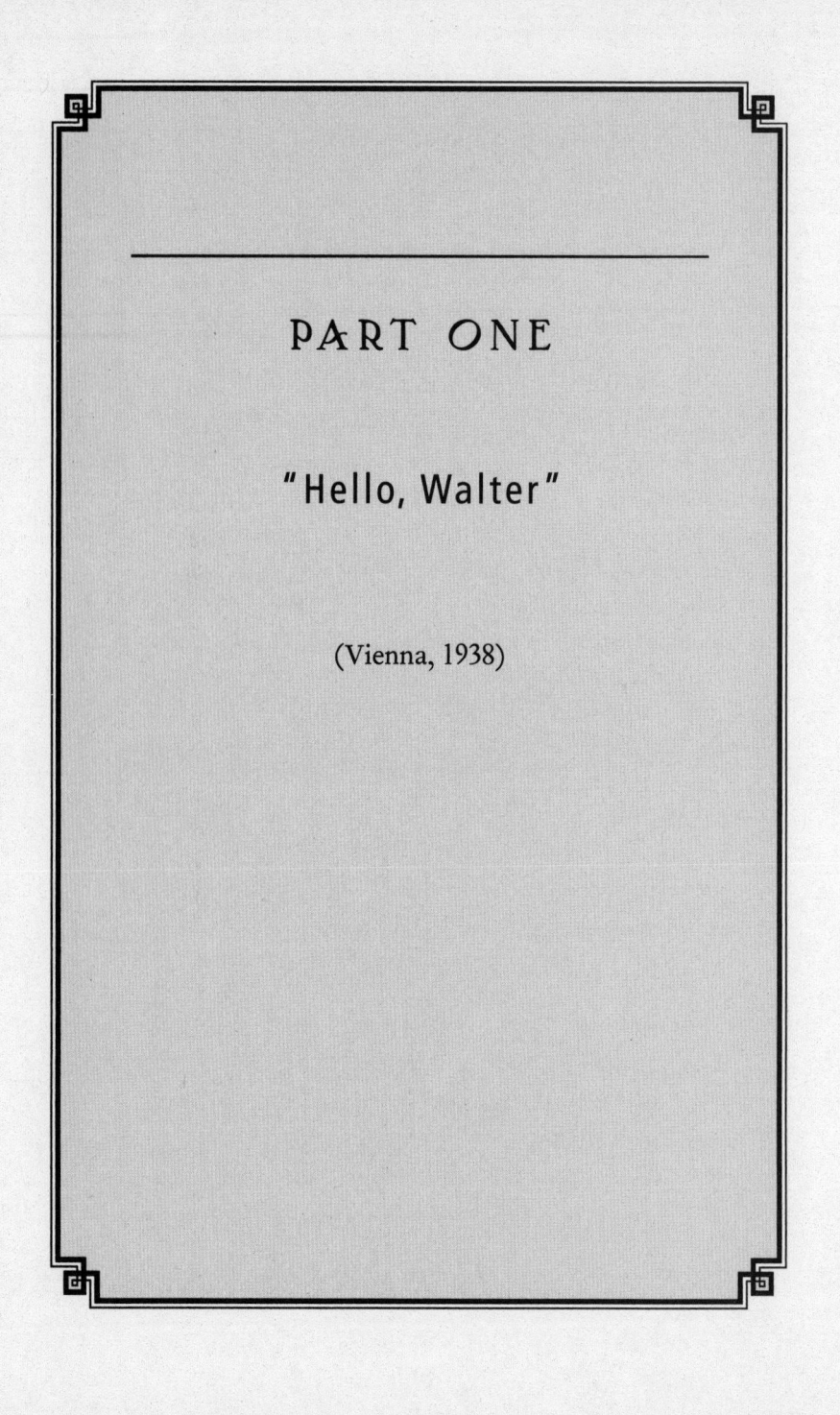

PART ONE

"Hello, Walter"

(Vienna, 1938)

1

Of course I'd seen him before. Many times. In the cafés, bars, restaurants, theaters, concert halls, and beautiful shops of a small city like Vienna, everyone knew who was who, and everyone knew who might one day be more than that.

I lived at a fashionable address: 11 Kohlmarkt, next to Demel, the famous patisserie. One lunchtime, I rushed out of my front door, looked back to wave good-bye to a friend, and bumped into Walter. For a moment, he held me close. Apologies. Laughter. He took my arm.

"We're going to have a glass of champagne, Trudi. This calls for a celebration."

It was a command, and I obeyed.

I am sitting on a gilt chair looking at him across one of the small, marble-topped tables at Demel.

"You're making hats?" Walter asks. "How's business? Surely a lady in your position should be in her salon, looking after her clients, not sitting in cafés having a good time."

"Are you lecturing me? Is that what we came here for? I work very hard—I'm entitled to a break. Anyway, you seem well informed."

"I've been watching you."

"Sir?" The waitress hands him the menu. Walter takes out his spectacles. "May I order for you, Trudi?"

I love the refined movements of his lips; his thick, shiny hair, graying at the temples; his olive skin. I have seen him glancing at me at the Café Rebhuhn. Once he left early, in a coat that was much too long. He looked pathetic. I think I began to love him then.

"Tell me about yourself. Are you happy?" he asks.

"I'm all right. You?"

"I'm lonely."

"You?" I laugh. "Lots of girls are after you. You're never alone."

"I didn't say that I was alone. I said I was lonely."

Our food arrives. Cold lobster, a huge green salad, champagne.

"You are young to have a broken marriage," Walter says. "I saw you the other day with Pepi."

"Do you know him?"

"Yes, and I like him a lot. Why do you want to divorce him?"

"Ask me why I married him."

"Why did you marry him?"

"I thought I was in love."

4

2

Demel's customers were the beau monde—famous, important, rich. It was the place to be seen, to stay au courant. We
went for elevenses, delicate snacks and pastries with cream;
we went for absinthe or a glass of champagne. We nibbled
Sachertorte at any time of day—a chocolate cake so fine that
it melted in our mouths. We went to Demel to watch the
great and the good, and of course, we went to gossip.

Demel was a place of old-fashioned courtesy. Hands
were kissed, heels respectfully clicked. Nobody was ever in
a hurry. Sometimes I took customers there or met friends
for coffee; at other times I just sat there alone, feeling privi-
leged. I admired the wine-colored carpets and window seats
where nests of little old ladies peeped out at passersby. Most
important! Because everybody knew everybody, and it was
delicious to know who was walking with whom.

I was here again, with Walter. The blue silk-covered walls
seem bluer, silkier. The richly draped brocade curtains seem
more sumptuous. The pair of large antique blackamoors in
their niches smile at me. Sparkling crystal chandeliers fairy
tale the room.

I wanted him. I was very young, and I had never wanted
anything so much. He was a successful businessman. His
apartment was elegant and comfortable; he had a beautiful
motorcar. I felt inadequate.

He said that he would ring the next day.

I waited by the window. Opposite was the building of the Vaterländische Front, Austria's nationalist party. It looked like any of the other large solid old buildings surrounding it. Anyone threatened by the Nazis felt it offered some protection. Not that the Vaterländische Front was on our side, exactly. But my enemy's enemy . . .

I wandered from room to room, thinking how lucky I was to live in this beautiful building. It had four floors, each one divided into two apartments. The ground floor was occupied by Hiess, a large luxury store. I rented both the apartments on the first floor. The one overlooking Kohlmarkt I had chosen for my home; the one at the back was my business premises. I had a hat salon with adjoining workrooms. Biedermeier furniture, silver-gray walls, curtains, and carpets. Three large, Chinese red, lacquer-framed mirrors. On the center table stood a round, white and gilt cage housing two lovebirds. The room was bright with sunlight. I could hear thunder in the distance. But who cared?

What if he doesn't ring? Is it true he has a girlfriend? Doris shouldn't have mentioned it. I pushed the thought away, but now it is back again, threatening me.

It is already six. I lift the receiver and put it down again. I pace my sitting room, cursing my friend, cursing Kohlmarkt, cursing Demel. I thought that I was attracted to him, sexually and otherwise, but it is more than that. Much more.

Suddenly the telephone rings.

Next day I meet Walter in a small café, one of those lovely

old-fashioned hideaways, a tiny, red-plushed place with lots of mirrors and no daylight. I wear a lilac chiffon dress; my hair is piled high.

Walter walks toward me. He smiles.

Tonight he will take me to dinner. I put on a white linen dress, white sandals. I carry an emerald green handbag. My red hair is held back by an emerald silk sash, tied at my neck. Its loose ends move in the wind.

Walter wears a dark gray bespoke flannel suit, handmade white brogues with black toes, a white silk shirt, a tie. No doubt all of this came from Knize, his tailor. How handsome he is.

He drives me in his open-top car to have dinner at a little restaurant in the Vienna woods. We sit in a garden, under old chestnut trees. Red and white gingham tablecloths, candlelight, icy white wine in carafes. He orders a liter of Riesling. The wine is very potent, very dry; the food is exquisite. Two blond peasant boys in lederhosen play the zither. They sing songs of love, of eyes, mouths, girls. *If you don't like my blue, blue bed, all right, that's fine / There are other girls like you / They're pretty too.*

His hand holds mine under the table, reaches for my knee. Summer breeze. The smell of wood, of pines, moss, living and dying. I like his choice of wine and food, the way he makes the waiters dance around us. The way he handles the night and me and the car. In the twilight his eyes are purple velvet.

From time to time moonlight breaks through. Tree trunks are overgrown with moss. Fallen leaves and twigs crackle as we drive through the dark, pine-scented wood. The birds have gone to sleep. I feel calm, sheltered, his arm around my shoulders.

A deer leaps over the shrubs, sweeps past us, stops, pirouettes, then elegantly dances up a hill and disappears. Walter stops the car. Was it a vision? We look at each other and smile.

Suddenly there is light, as if someone with a long taper has lit an old-fashioned gas lamp. Glowworms, yards of them close together on moss, form an illuminated carpet. A few yards away, another carpet, and another.

"It's magic, Walter. I have to see it close."

Worms, hundreds of them—fat little phosphorescent worms, motionless. Cold white lights.

"Why are they here? What makes them lie like this?"

Walter takes my hands. Silent, unsmiling, we stand close to one another, filled with longing. He runs his fingers through my hair. He knows how to kiss. A breeze weaves through the branches of the old trees. Leaves shiver.

I stand undressed in my blue bedroom, full of warmth and the ecstasy of young love. That night was crammed with excitement, shreds of sleep. He visits my dreams. Kisses fly in all directions. I try to catch them with my green butterfly net.

The first time you came to No. 11, you were very shy. I wanted you to feel at home. I had straightened the rugs, again and again. They moved if they lay on top of a fitted carpet, always in the same direction. I had polished the candlesticks. On the windowsill were the red roses you had sent me. I thought that it might look too obvious, and I put them on the table. I turned off the lights and opened the windows wide. It was a warm night. The gaslight of the streetlamp turned your roses crimson.

You sat on the sofa, ill at ease, looking at me. I, in the armchair, far away, longed for you. We drank wine; I wasn't used to it. I moved closer to you.

After you died, I kept your wardrobe locked, with all your clothes inside, all your lovely ties. The scent of you. I sat inside this wardrobe when I missed you so much.

3

More and more frightening news filtered across the German border. All Jewish money and property confiscated. Concentration camps. Torture. *I don't believe it,* I lied to myself.

In love with a city? Yes. I was in love with Vienna, where I was born. Its calm, its charm, its old houses, every corner of every street. Even in the early thirties, when many Viennese were poor and unemployed, I found its magic irresistible. So did Walter.

One summer day he came in his car to show me the sights of imperial Vienna. I didn't want to go. It was unbearably hot. But he stood there, so eager, his eyes shining. I put on my walking shoes and a cool cotton dress.

We made the rounds. Churches, monuments, palaces— Walter knew all their stories: the year they were built, by whom, how long it had taken to finish them, everything. I looked at his lovely happy face, saw how proud he was to share all this with me.

"And of course you know our Stephansdom," he said, pointing at the cathedral. "It marks the center of the city. Do you know anything else about it?"

I didn't, and I was too hot to care. "Tell me," I said.

"It was built in 1147; completely destroyed in 1258 by a fire—it was so hot it melted the bells. Incredibly, in 1290, it happened again. That same year, the complete rebuilding began."

I was tired, longing for a cold drink, and remembered a café in a side street. Almost in front of the door stood a horse, staring stoically ahead. I have always been afraid of horses and I pulled Walter away.

He walked in front of me, toward the car. I looked at the perfect shape of his head. The thought that he was mine made me feel unbearably happy.

The magnificent State Opera House, Vienna's pride. Walking up marble stairs, across inlaid marble floors. Waltzes by

Lanner and Strauss. The whisper of silk crinolines still lingers. The ceilings, painted by artists of centuries past, are lit up by rows of crystal chandeliers which spark off tiny lights. Millions and millions of them. Like diamonds. Like a fairy tale. Every evening at the opera is a glittering, unforgettable occasion. Especially just before midnight on New Year's Eve, when the bells of St. Stephan start to ring out.

Walter showed me the nineteenth-century parliament building. "Lit from inside, it looks like Brussels lace," he said. We looked at the Karlskirche, with its domed copper roof that has turned green—the oldest baroque building in Austria. The Votivkirche, its soaring spires rising into the dark sky. We went to the fairground. Finally we sat down in a garden restaurant, ate Vienna sausages, drank iced lager. Then through fields and woods stretching down to the Danube. Flowering trees, the old-fashioned amusement park, and the famous Ferris wheel. The Danube—never blue, but a lovely, old, busy, dirty gray river, cutting Vienna in two.

His arm around my shoulders, Walter asks, "Have you ever taken a cruise down the Danube to Wachau?"

"No."

"Let's go together. You will see the loveliest river valley in Europe. Imagine—old castles perched on craggy rocks. Gilded baroque churches dotted across the green banks. It's fabulous in spring, when the trees are in bloom. I know you will love it."

We were young, and the world was ours. Viennese music and all the people who loved it so much were ours. In the morning they sing; upstairs, downstairs, on the bus, in the metro, humming in the streets. Up on the fourth floor a window cleaner whistles the Radetzky March.

The Austrians love wine, women, and song. I remember the white wines. Easy to drink, they flow too easily down your throat. Fruity, dry wines, delicious with chicken fried in bread crumbs.

We walked some more, until I could go no farther. My face red and hot, my hair in a state, my feet sore, I cried.

"I've had enough, Walter. I need to sit down."

He apologized, pinched my cheek, and took me to a tavern in a cellar next to the cathedral. It was cool there. The food was good, the wine chilled.

Walter loved small, intimate bars. There were many of them all over Vienna. He took me to his favorite.

How many girls had he taken there before? Beautiful girls.

He calls for me, looking handsome in his navy blue mohair suit and white shirt. I have been to the hairdresser. I try to look my best.

The bar is enchanting. Dark red velvet curtains, bright red linen tablecloth. Candlelight reflected by mirrored walls. The pianist plays romantic music. We dance very close to one another. In the dim light my eyes meet the veiled eyes of the man dancing next to me. The pianist's gaze burns through my clothes.

Walter notices. He falls silent. We never go there again.

4

I waited for Walter in his flat. Until I took the receiver off the hook, the telephone rang constantly. Girls. There would be little notes when we got into his car outside his building: *I still live at No. 7, Susie. I waited, Lilli. Cheri, encore? Hughette.* The telephone number of a young lady called Carolle.

No wonder, my darling, no wonder they were after you. No wonder. Your eyes, the blue of African violets, dark hair, graying at the temples. Your slightly olive skin, smooth all over your body. Your sweetness, kindness, decency. You *did* flirt, trade on your good looks, but not like a rogue. Good-naturedly, for fun. Of course I was jealous. You grinned at girls, a twinkle in your eye.

There was a photograph of a beautiful woman in the drawer of your desk.

"Who is she, Walter?"

"A past love."

That was all you said. I wanted to ask: *How long ago? What color is her hair? Her eyes? Her complexion? Is she tall, slim, with beautiful legs? Beautiful hands? Is she a threat to me?* But I didn't.

I am civil to him, but I don't like him, Walter's so-called friend. Poldi interferes. He wants Walter to marry an heiress, a young woman living in the same building. Poldi is clever. Romanian. He is a short-legged, broad-shouldered little man, head three sizes too large, glittering black eyes. He is overdressed. Poldi means trouble.

"Trudi, Walter asked me to talk to you." My heart misses a beat. "Mira tried to commit suicide."

Mira? Who is Mira? The girl in the photograph in Walter's desk?

"Who's Mira?" I ask. He watches me, savors my shock. I am strong. I will deny him that pleasure. The yellow walls of my sitting room are turning around. The patterns of the blue Chinese carpet explode. I remain cool.

"She is a divorcée," he explains, "and for the last two years, on and off, Walter was having an affair with her. Until he met you."

"Why has Walter never told me about her?"

"Obvious, isn't it? He didn't want to upset you. He tried several times to break it off with her, but she wouldn't let him go."

"And now? What is going to happen? Is he going back to her? Why has he sent you? Why doesn't he tell me himself?"

"She is dead."

Good.

No. I mustn't think that. It's terrible.

But it *is* good. Now she can't take him away from me.

Or can she? Will her death come between us?

Finally I realize Poldi is still talking. "Did you hear me, Trudi? She's dead."

* * *

When I heard the full story from Walter, I was angry at first. Very angry. And then sorry. But what a trick.

Mira lived with her widowed mother on the fourth floor of one of those big old buildings in the center of Vienna. It was Easter Monday. After lunch her mother went to visit her sister. Mira was going out, too and asked her mother to make sure she was home by seven at the latest, telling her it was important because she was expecting a telephone call and might not be able to get back in time for it herself.

But Mother *was* late. She came home and found Mira on the bed, unconscious, a letter next to her. A few sleeping tablets on the pillow, the empty bottle on the floor. She rushed out to get help and accidentally locked her keys inside the flat. Easter Monday. No locksmiths. Eventually, the fire brigade arrived. Their ladders didn't reach the fourth floor. They had to use a battering ram on the heavy front door. Mira was still alive. Four hours later she died in the hospital. Poor, beautiful Mira, whom I never knew. Her plan didn't come off.

Walter holds me tight. Should I cry?

It took a lot of tact, patience, and love to reestablish the equilibrium that had existed between us before the tragedy.

5

I have influenza. Walter sits on the edge of my bed, holding my hand. He is not afraid to catch my cold. I am hot. I shiver.

Red roses. Lots of them. Walter is generous; he always gives me red roses. Their color matches my Bokhara rug, contrasts well with the blue walls, painted to look like moiré silk. The roses stand in a tall crystal vase. I like to see the long stems in clear water.

Mother arrives unexpectedly. I know she likes him, and why not? He is kind, tactful, modest, well behaved. Mother adores beautiful people. She sits on a chair at my little desk, still glamorous, very chic. Her famous dimpled smile appears. It is used only for special people.

Walter looks at me. We exchange smiles. They get on well, Mother and Walter. I am happy, but hot. Their voices are faint.

"Trudi." Walter's voice brings me back. "May I come tomorrow?" Good God, what a question!

I nod and fall asleep. Mother is still there when I wake up. She smiles at me.

"Has he gone?" I ask.

"Yes, darling," she says. "Don't worry. He will be back. You know, Trudi, when I saw those eyes, I knew."

"Knew what, Mother?" We laugh. "Would you like a drink? Coffee?"

"No, thank you. I don't want anything. You rest. I'll stay. Later on, I'll make you a hot drink."

I close my eyes. I remember my parents and I walking alongside a cornfield. I was a little girl. It was a summer's day; I could almost hear the air vibrate with heat. Brushed by a sudden breeze, the ripe fruit inside the heads of corn rattled softly, like maracas. At the end of the field stood a huge oak tree, still clad in its leaves. The grass underneath was losing its green. I ran backward and forward, picking cornflowers for my mother. Poppies, daisies, and a few stems of golden corn.

She smiled when I gave them to her. I loved her. A love that lasted all my life. Suddenly I realized how beautiful she was. Soft face, warm hair, shaded gold; large eyes, the color and sparkle of well-cut sapphires. I saw that people smiled at her; I was envious and tried to copy her. I tried, like her, to walk with a slight sway of my hips. I didn't succeed and was upset. No one looked at me.

Mother was aware of the glances from passersby and occasionally turned her head to look at Father, with a big grin and a twinkle in her eye. Arm in arm, they laughed together, talked together, walked together. No one looked at me.

The wind rustled in the trees. Leaves fluttered.

I adored my dark-haired, dark-eyed father. He came from a long line of jewelers. He was a specialist in copying and restoring antique jewelry. He had taste, style, and the beautiful, long, slim hands of an artist. He walked with a beautifully straight back until the end of his days.

He could do no wrong in my eyes. I always took his part, even against my mother. Yet when I had an argument with her, he would stab me in the back, staunchly on her side. But no matter how many times it happened, I felt no bitterness. My loyalty to him never failed. They were lovebirds—but lovebirds can't live without each other. If one of them dies, the other dies, too. Not so in their case. Life had decided differently.

I recovered from the fever. Walter and my mother became friends. She adored him.

6

February 1938: Walter, some friends, and I walked across Graben. A young, shabbily dressed man shouted at us. He cursed us, baring his teeth. We took no notice and walked on. He smelled of drink. He shouted after us, "Jews! Dirty Jews!" and raised his fist. Walter swiveled around, jumped at him like a tiger. The man ran.

A small bomb exploded in a telephone kiosk. It caused hardly any damage, but it worried me. Austrians were not normally aggressive. Was it wise to go to Paris now? To produce a new collection? Walter advised me not to change my plans. Everyone persuaded me to go.

At the beginning of March 1938, I flew to Paris to do my buying for the coming season. There, the main topic of conversation was the trouble in Austria.

I sat in a bistro, having coffee and croissants for breakfast. I saw the headline in the previous day's *Paris-Soir:* DR. KURT SCHUSCHNIGG LOSES HIS FIGHT. I bought a newspaper. The Germans were ready to march into Austria, just waiting for Hitler's command.

Alone, scared, I ran back to my hotel and started to telephone. My friends and business contacts confirmed the terrifying news.

"No, no, madame," said the young lady at the blockmaker's. Her black eyes opened wide in shock. *"Ne revenez pas à Vienne, madame! Jamais! C'est impossible. C'est très, très dangereux. Restez ici, madame, chez nous."*

My buying agent, Monsieur Roubach, an elderly, kind man, spoke English. He had never forgiven the Germans for emptying his precious wine cellar.

"Oh no, madame," he said. "Never can you go back to Vienna. Never!" He sliced his hand across his throat. "Grrr!" he said, and his head began to tremble. "You will stay with us! Yes? Madame Roubach *et mes enfants,* they will have honor."

Madame Paulette and her directrice were my friends. "Out of the question," Paulette said authoritatively, putting her manicured hand under my chin. "We wouldn't let you go." Her normally businesslike voice was warm. "So young," said the directrice. Her watery blue eyes were sad.

Early next morning, I booked a car and Monsieur Roubach for the next two days. I told him to arrange appointments back-to-back, during lunchtime and after hours. I visited every leading house, bought all the materials I needed, and met with all my fashion contacts to hear what they were thinking.

Then I telephoned my friend Marie-Louise, a model at Patou. I knew that she was having an affair with a minister in the French government. She might know something about Hitler and Austria.

In the late afternoon of 9 March, I waited for her outside the Café de la Paix. I sat on a small metal chair at a round metal table, a little stove next to it, as with every Paris café when the weather is not yet warm.

Marie-Louise strode across the rue de la Paix. Her understated elegance was dramatic. A tight-fitting gray tweed suit molded her sleek, sexy body. A sable scarf protected her from the slight chill. We embraced, happy to see each other. We ordered coffee and aperitifs. As always, Café de la Paix was busy, people coming and going, shouting at one another in different languages.

"Trudi," she said, "you must stay in Paris. You can't go back to Vienna. Whatever happens."

So she knows, I thought.

"There is no choice. I want you alive. Stay with me. Don't worry about money."

"How can I stay here?" I asked. "Walter and my parents are in Vienna. If they are in trouble, I want to be with them."

"Trudi, darling. We'll think of something. Maybe Pierre

will know what to do." Her smile would have cheered the saddest person. It didn't cheer me. I envied her fresh, rosy complexion. Her security. Large emerald and diamond earrings matched her green eyes.

I returned to my hotel. After a little rest, a bath, and a change of clothes, I went out again. I wanted to walk through Paris by myself. To see its people, its shops. Feel its freedom. *Liberté, Egalité, Fraternité.*

7

It was twilight. I walked toward la place de la Concorde. Hundreds and hundreds of black lampposts surrounded it. Octagonal glass shapes. Old-fashioned, romantic. They shimmered, sparkled; they took me into another world. It was impossible to imagine that, once, the guillotine had stood there. On the left, the green gardens of the Louvre. On the right, the flowering gardens of the Champs-Elysées. I found a quiet corner to stop and take it all in, maybe for the last time.

I walked up the Champs-Elysées, past majestic buildings and beautiful shopwindows. Café after café, people sat outside, eating, drinking, enjoying themselves. An endless stream. The comparison with what was happening to people at home was unbearable.

I arrived at Le Rond Point.

A young couple, hand in hand, was mesmerized by the four fountains. They seemed to have forgotten their baby girl in the pram. Black eyes, black curls, white coat with pearl buttons. She was fascinated by the twinkling drops of water and glittering lights. I tickled her under her chin. She closed her soft baby fist around my finger and cooed. Her tiny presence changed my mood. *Maybe it won't be as bad as everybody thinks,* I thought. *Please God, help us.*

I was tired and hungry. Fouquet's, the fashionable place to go, was close by. At the next table was a young American couple who looked as though they were on their honeymoon. People spoke Spanish, Italian, German.

"*Mademoiselle?*" asked the waiter. I ordered *omelette aux champignons,* a salad. Melon.

"*Et pour boire, mademoiselle?*"

"*Du bière froide.*"

I ate some bread and excellent unsalted butter. My omelette arrived. Deliciously hot, beautifully presented.

I walked on, past la place de l'Étoile to l'arc de Triomphe. Majestic. Dignified. I missed Walter's explanations.

Early next morning Marie-Louise told me that her friend the minister would do everything in his power to get permission for Walter and my parents to come to France. She urged me again not to go back to Austria. To bring my family to Paris.

I telephoned Walter. My eyes filled with tears when I heard his voice.

"Trudi, darling."

"Walter, speak up. I can't hear you. Hello! He Hello! Hello—hello!" The line went dead. I dialec

"We were interrupted," he said. "Tell me how you are."

"Walter, you *must* come to Paris. At once."

"Why? What's happened?"

"Please come. Come as you are. No time to pack." My hands were shaking. Tears ran down my cheeks. "Walter, please. Listen to me. I've seen the papers. The French papers. Schuschnigg has lost. You're in danger—"

"Nonsense," he said. His voice was calm.

"The Germans are preparing to march into Austria! It's *certain.*"

"Don't be so pessimistic! Do your buying as usual, and come home. Come home to me."

"For God's sake, listen to me!"

Walter did not answer.

To go back to Vienna now would be a great gamble, yet I knew Walter would never survive on his own. He was no fighter.

I boarded the night plane to Vienna. I looked through the window of my plane. Down there was Paris—drama, fashion, elegance.

Good-bye, Paris, I whispered. *Good-bye, Lautrec. Good-bye fashion shows, wonderful food, avenues and boulevards, beautiful churches, picturesque houses with wooden shutters, organ grinders, spring breezes, the reflection of ancient walls in the Seine. Good-bye.*

I arrived in Vienna early in the morning of 11 March 1938. Walter met me at the airport. I felt his arms around me. His lips on mine. It was good to see him. Good not to be alone.

8

I went back to work. I loved my workroom, its atmosphere, my girls. There was Betty, with the face of a truck driver and the soul of an angel; she never had much to say but was always ready to help. Little Dolly: big, dark blue eyes, always laughing, luscious and plump; she ate horse-meat steak on Sundays as a treat. Anne-Marie, the girl with the best figure in the room, had never seen herself naked; as a devout Catholic, she believed to do so would be a sin, and took her bath wearing a nightdress.

I can still see my workroom. Starting under the window and stretching almost the full length of the room stood a wooden table seating twelve milliners. Every girl had a box of pins, a cushion with needles, a pair of scissors, and several thimbles. On the floor beside each chair was a cardboard box holding necessities for the work in hand. Spools of cotton in every color were slid onto a metal rod on legs that ran the whole length of the table. It was fixed at one end and locked at the other. That way, spools couldn't disappear. We had wig stands in various sizes. They were used to shape the hats. Against the wall was a table with gas rings, large and small irons, and a steam kettle.

There were straw braids in pastel shades and straw braids in bright colors. Velvets and silks; flowers, feathers, and ribbons. Order sheets, pieces of veiling, and other fabric were randomly pinned to the wall. Hats were everywhere: large hats, small hats, sports hats, and sophisticated turbans for evening. The place was almost a replica of the Paris workroom where I spent two months learning French hat design and techniques. Its directrice was a chic, slim woman with shrewd, penetrating eyes.

"Mademoiselle," she said, "you like to learn from the *modiste Parisienne*? Well, mademoiselle, never, never do you forget. The hat must be designed with the luxury, with the wit, and with the craftsmanship. Always it must be charming and amusing."

It was 1935. The poor were getting poorer; the rich, richer. As always, fashion catered to the rich. And French fashion was a dictatorship. Hats became smaller and smaller. More charming. More amusing. This was the time when a feather and a sequin was a hat.

My workroom glittered. It was alive. It took possession of me, made me forget the world outside. Everyone was busy, everyone was happy, chatting and laughing. The whole place reeked of fashion.

But this time, as I entered my beloved workroom, I felt

immediately that something had changed. The girls greeted me with politeness, but without the usual bright smiles and hellos. The usual questions were missing—*How was Paris, madame? What are the new hats like? Again small toques? Or do we have brims for a change? Did you have fun?* They were reserved—only slightly, but it was impossible to overlook. I pretended not to notice, thinking that I understood the reason for it. But I was wrong. They had not been influenced—yet—by Hitler's propaganda. For the moment, they were afraid for me, and embarrassed. They didn't know how to behave. They didn't want to hurt my feelings.

"Madame, may I speak to you?" my forelady asked.

"Of course, Stefanie."

"In private?"

Her voice was a tone higher than usual. She was tiny, ash-blond, with dark eyes.

"Come on, Steffi." I put my arm around her shoulders. "Let's go to my room, it's cozy there. Come, sit down. Tell me what the matter is."

"I don't know, madame. It's hard to explain. I can't understand it myself. While you were away, in those few days, everything changed."

Her eyes were bright with tears. "You shouldn't have come back! You shouldn't! I hoped you wouldn't. You were safe in Paris. Don't you know, any moment now, German troops will march into Austria!"

"How do you know?"

"My brother is a member of the Communist Party, and they are well informed. I worry about him just as much as I worry about you."

"I read the papers in Paris. Believe me, the world knows far more about our troubles than we do."

"So why did you come back? *Why?*"

"Steffi, you love your husband. I couldn't possibly abandon Walter. You understand."

She started to cry. "It's not so much what has actually happened. It's what is *going* to happen. Hitler isn't even here, but suddenly everyone is a Nazi. They've all been members of the Party for a long time. They don't hide their swastika pins anymore—they wear them openly. Proudly."

"Steffi, don't worry so much. Not everybody is bad. I am sure there are plenty of people like you."

She looked at me anxiously. While I was away, Chancellor Schuschnigg had called a referendum on Austria retaining her autonomy. He wanted to see the people's loyalty. All day long, youngsters paraded up and down the Kärntnerstrasse. On the left side of the street, the Socialists were shouting, "*Heil* Schuschnigg!" On the right, the Nazis screamed, "*Heil* Hitler!"

"And who do you think I saw on the Nazi side, wearing a swastika pin and shouting?"

"Who?"

"Our two little learners, our two little nobodies—Pauline and Anna."

That really shook me. It hurt. I flew back to the workroom and started shouting at the two girls—hard, angry words, in front of everyone. Then I walked away, wishing I could undo what I had done.

A few days later, there was a knock at my door. In those days, a knock at the door could mean the beginning of the end.

"Come in," I said.

A huge bunch of flowers appeared first—with two pairs of eyes peeping through. Pauline and Anna. Only fifteen, Pauline was like a young deer—slim, with long, delicate legs, dark, calm eyes. Anna was a country bumpkin.

"Frau Trudi," Pauline whispered. "We have come to tell you not to worry. We are members of the Nazi Party, and we have told our friends in our group how nice and kind you are. They promised to protect you. Nothing bad will happen to you."

PART TWO

Swastika Flags

(Vienna, 1938)

1

The eyes of the dictator across the border were fixed on the land of his birth. Long ago, Hitler had stated that German Austria must return to the Great German Fatherland. People of one blood belonged together in one reich.

Austria was invaded, occupied, annexed, and made a province of Germany during the course of one week in March 1938.

It had become clear that any intervention by the guaranteeing powers—England, France, and Italy—was unlikely. Dr. Schuschnigg made desperate attempts to stop the German Reich's bid to annex Austria, but to no avail. The referendum he called was intended to show the world that Austrians wanted their country to be free and independent, Christian and united. But it was too late. By 13 March, polling day, the flags of Nazi Germany were already flying over Austria. On 15 March, Hitler declared it an integral part of Germany.

* * *

11 March 1938. Eight p.m. Dr. Kurt Schuschnigg, the Federal Chancellor, addressed the Austrian nation. He began his speech with his back turned toward his colleagues and opponents. He spoke facing his own empty office.

"Men and women of Austria. Today we face a difficult and fateful situation."

He told us that the German government had presented him with an ultimatum, requiring him to appoint a government approved by them. If he failed to comply, German troops would cross the border.

He continued: "I declare before all the world that reports of workers' riots, of rivers of blood, of a government not in control of the situation and unable to maintain law and order, are pure invention. Our president has instructed me to inform the Austrian nation that we are yielding to force. Because we are resolved on no account to spill blood, we have ordered our armed forces, in the event of an invasion by the German army, to offer no resistance."

He ended his speech by saying, "And so I take leave of the Austrian people at this hour with a heartfelt wish: God protect Austria!" His voice shook.

I could hear shouts in the street.

Hitler's orders:

> The conduct of the troops must give the impression
> that we have no desire to wage war against our brother
> nation. It is in our interests that the whole operation

should be carried out without the use of force in the
form of a peaceful entry, welcomed by the population.
Therefore any provocation is to be avoided. If, however,
resistance is offered, it must be broken ruthlessly by
force of arms.

The freedom and even the lives of supporters of the ex-
Chancellor, of resolute opponents of National Socialism,
and of the hundreds of thousands of Jewish citizens of
Austria, were now called into question. On the night of 11
March, squads of Nazis rampaged through the city. People
were dragged from their homes and flung into requisitioned
houses. Others were placed under house arrest. A dark week
in a darkening world had begun.

At three minutes past midnight on 12 March, German
troops crossed the Austrian border—a disaster marching
toward us. Marching, marching, marching. Droning planes.
One hundred thousand soldiers. Armored cars. Tanks.

A deadly silence covered the land.

We hear it, coming from the end of the street. Closer, closer.
Each step at the same split second. Each step the same length,
loud, powerful, terrifying. We are like tiny ants whose nest
has been disturbed, running in all directions, trying to find a
hole, a blade of grass, somewhere—anywhere—to hide.

Darkness. Walter and I crouch on the floor of my hat
salon. No lights, strangled radio. We hold hands. Mirrors
reflect streetlamps. My hats, in their large display cases, seem

ridiculous, frivolous. In the dim light, the silver-gray walls and carpets, so elegant, look ghostly and drab.

"Don't worry, darling. Don't worry. Please." Walter's voice is a cracked whisper. "Everything will be all right."

"Walter, how can it possibly be all right?"

He squeezes my hand.

They are coming closer still. I don't cry. Walter puts his arm around my shoulders, pulls me toward him. He, too, wants to feel close, to hold me tightly. For how much longer will we have each other?

Tramp tramp tramp.

My hands tighten around his. We have waited hour upon hour; followed the German advance on the radio step by step, town after town after town, across the whole of our undefended country. Poor Austria. Poor deceived Austrians. Poor defenseless Jews. Now the boots stop. What will they do? Take us from our homes? They have stopped outside the building of the Vaterländische Front, their greatest and most dangerous enemy in Austria. The streets are packed with Nazi supporters—hysterical people. Dangerous people.

Shrieking, screaming, screeching of stopped cars. Shouted commands, running motors. Every scream, every shout seems directed at us. Oh, God, how frightened I am.

Then sudden quiet, followed by howls. Shattered glass, splintered wood.

"They're smashing up the building," Walter whispers.

The lava of hatred erupts.

Kicking boots leave at three a.m.

We dare not look out of the window. We are still on the floor, in the dark. They may have left guards behind. They might see us.

"Walter, we have to get out. Immediately."

There is a pause.

"Do you mean now? As we are?"

"Yes."

"In the middle of the night?"

"Yes, in the middle of the night. *Now.* Darling, you don't seem to understand the danger we're in."

"Trudi, where do you want to go? And how? We have no money. The banks are closed."

"We have enough money to buy tickets to Czechoslovakia, and when we get there your family will help us. And we have my jewelry. Walter, please, listen to me. You know my brother-in-law, Otto? Two days ago, he crossed the Czech border. He left his family behind. He's a well-known industrialist, and he was afraid he might be arrested at the frontier and implicate them. When he was safely across, he telephoned Julie and told her to pack her jewelry, nothing else, and follow him with the children. They are safe now."

Walter touches my cheek. Our eyes meet.

"This afternoon, Frau von Alpenheim came to the salon to pay her bill. She advised me to leave, and leave soon. She said I was running out of time. That she knows what Hitler has planned for the Jews. That no one can imagine what is going to happen, and that no one will be able to help us. She wouldn't say more than that, she just kept telling me to get out, looking me straight in the eye. And you want to wait? Wait for what, Walter?"

The answer came slowly. "You know that you always put your head down and charge at the wall, whereas I need to think carefully before I make a decision. Let's make arrangements and leave in an organized way, openly. We are not going to flee under cover of darkness, like criminals. Trust me. The Nazis have a lot to do, consolidating the occupation. The things that *we* fear will come later."

"Walter! How can—"

"Trudi, you are forgetting—what will happen to your parents? They have no one to advise them, no money. They are helpless. Will you leave them? Without saying good-bye? Without making arrangements for them?"

Of course, Walter was right. Except that neither of us expected the world to act as it did. Later that same day, the frontiers of neighboring countries were closed to refugees from Austria. We were trapped.

2

12 March 1938: My eyes won't open. My brain is paralyzed. Daylight brings back nightmares. I reach for his hand. He isn't there.

"Walter!"

He's gone. He has gone back to his apartment to check on things. What has happened? Oh, God. I crawl under my blanket again. I have to think for both of us. Act for both of us.

I get up and go to my bathroom, avoiding looking in the mirror. The sky is cloudless, almost Mediterranean blue.

I make coffee, go back to bed. It is empty. The room, the flat, everything is empty without him.

I brush my hair. Long, wild red hair—Walter's pride. Who will sleep here, after we have gone, in this lovely pale blue and cream bedroom? The windows look out on Vienna's first sky-scraper. At night, when all the lights are on, it looks roman-tic. The windows of my drawing room face Kohlmarkt. I can't look out there, not on my own. The Nazis have smashed the building that protected us.

Nobody will come today. It is an undeclared day of mourning. Everything has changed. Overnight we lost our country. Without a fight. Being Jewish, we are fair game, unprotected by law. They will take everything from us. They will hurt us. They have done it already in Germany. Children cried. Wives pleaded. They were kicked in the stomach. Tears mixed with vomit. Neighbors turned to stone. *Don't you see, Walter? Don't you see? We must run.*

The next day, and the day after that, no one came to work. And then I screwed up my courage and went downstairs, out of the door, and into the street. I took one look around and went back inside. My heart thundered in my ears. Kohlmarkt

37

was empty, as quiet as if the plague had struck. Enormous red flags with swastikas—hundreds, thousands—had been hung closely across the street, from one end of Kohlmarkt to the other; they formed a ceiling, blocking out everything. There was no sun, just swastika flags. No sky, just swastika flags. There was no God.

The shock slowly disappeared, but I feel gripped by a thick, sticky feeling. It paralyzes me. Sticking to my hands; I can't work. To my legs; I can't walk. To my brain; I can't think or sleep. Fear fills my black dreams, turning them round and round, sitting heavily on my chest. I can't breathe.

Few people know the real meaning of fear, its hopeless, crushing effect. Fear had been in me for a long time. This indescribable atmosphere. There was something hovering over me, urging me. What did I do? I carried on, stubbornly, pretending to be deaf. Stupid? Of course, but helpless, too. I was in love. No changes, please. No yesterdays, no tomorrows. I was a coward.

Not anymore. I scrutinize myself with critical eyes. Is it just a front? Is there a crushed face under the mask? No, I am strong now. I will do everything possible to make sure we escape.

3

14 March 1938: Jews were not allowed to wear swastika pins. This was the privilege of party members only. Every person without one was fair game. It seemed grotesque that a quarter inch of silver metal had so much power. I had made an appointment for 14 March with my lawyer to sign some important papers. I *had* to go, and I had to go without a swastika pin.

"Why don't you take Pauline with you?" Walter suggested. Arm in arm, we were soon on our way: me, Pauline, swastika pin.

On our way back, from across the road, we saw a crowd of people in front of the Vaterländische Front, staring at the pavement, white-faced and still.

Cars stopped; people stopped. A crowd quickly formed. The silence was occasionally broken by sharp commands.

We went closer. Young girls, young boys, old men, and old women on their knees were scrubbing the pavement. A girl of about ten held a big brush in her bleeding hand. "Acid," someone whispered. "There is more acid than water in those buckets." I smelled it. However hard the people on their knees scrubbed, the writing in red paint wouldn't come off. The brown-shirted youngsters jumped onto their cracked, bleeding hands to remind them and the Austrian nation who was the master.

A woman vomited into her handkerchief. Men turned their heads away.

A shaft of sunlight shot past them and lingered farther down the road. People came out of shops and quickly went back in again. For a split second the face of an old man appeared at a window. It was too much, even for those who had welcomed the invading army.

Before the invasion, illegal Austrian Nazis had painted the pavements outside the Vaterländische Front with slogans: DOWN WITH JEWS. KILL THE PARASITES. *HEIL* HITLER. Members of the Vaterländische Front had painted their own slogans: HITLER IS A HOMICIDAL MANIAC. DOWN WITH HITLER AND HIS NAZI THUGS.

The shocked Jews, plucked from the street at random, had to scrub off these slogans. Not one of them showed any emotion. Not a tear was shed, not even by the children. They kept on scrubbing. They kept on scrubbing long after the masters had left, but the paint could not be removed, and eventually, one by one, they shuffled off.

No one knew what was going to happen. Were we allowed out? Was it dangerous? Gradually we dared to use the telephone, hoping that the Gestapo were not listening in. We spoke in short sentences. Even innocuous things were conveyed in riddles.

Mother telephoned. I could hardly hear her. She tried to tell me that they were worried about their daughter. Newspapers had reported the scenes at Kohlmarkt. She was so careful with her words that not even I could understand her.

"Trudi," she said. "You know, the daughter . . . Yes, the newspapers, you know. She, you know who I mean. We worry. Ask her, yes? Ask her."

I finally understood what she meant and told her there was no reason to be alarmed, that her daughter was perfectly all right. Father came on the line to hear for himself. His voice a little choked, he said only, "Darling."

A wave of love rose up inside me. Insecure and helpless, any kind word or sign of affection shook me.

Pepi's mother telephoned. "Trudi, we worry about you in the middle of it all. Come to us. You know where your home is. I have your room ready."

Then Pepi himself: "Mother and Father want you to stay with us. Please come, even if we are apart. Extraordinary times warrant extraordinary behavior. It is better here. Don't stay there on your own. Please come."

How could I tell them that I was not on my own?

Friends telephoned. They thought I was in the middle of a battlefield.

Walter and I stayed at home for the next few days. Slowly, slowly, friends appeared again. Customers. After much persuasion, my parents.

Walter had been right again. For the moment, we were being left alone.

4

Pepi was a brilliant tap dancer, the best I had seen onstage. He had extended his dance units to twelve bars instead of the standard eight and had a very fast pair of feet. He was very witty, and always laughing. To him, the world was one solid lump of fun. He was never serious, never depressed, never pessimistic. It sounds lovely, but it wasn't. Permanent sunshine, permanent heat. Without a cloud, or the relief of cool rain?

My skinny, long-boned father, who carried himself with great elegance, came to visit us at No. 11, his left arm in a sling.

"Don't worry, children, don't worry." With an impish smile he said, "This is only for protection." He took the sling off as Walter helped him out of his coat. "They won't take an elderly man with his arm in a sling, will they?"

"Oh, Father! Elderly? You're fifty-three! You're just a boy!"

Like all the older Austrian intellectuals, he spoke with a slight touch of Viennese slang. Poor Father. I ruffled his dark, graying hair, looked into his brown eyes, filled with his family's strength of character. He went straight to his favorite chair, which was deep enough to make himself and his long legs comfortable. Sitting on the floor next to him, I said, "Where's Mother? Why didn't she come with you?"

"She's afraid. She said she could not stand by and see

someone behave disrespectfully to me. She doesn't want to end up in prison."

They were such passionate people, my parents.

The doorbell went. Pepi, a grin on his face, arrived in time for coffee. But the grin had an edge to it. I knew Pepi.

"What is it?" I asked. "Why are you laughing?"

He glanced at me and looked away again. "They got me this morning."

I looked at his warm face, retroussé nose, his freckles and toothy smile.

"What do you mean, they got you? Who? Where? Why?"

"The Nazis." He danced to the table, took his coffee, and walked over to sit with Walter on the sofa. "I came from the Leopoldstadt. As I walked across the Danube Bridge, four Brownshirts stopped me. 'What is your religion?' one asked. 'Jewish,' I answered. He gave me a long street broom, you know, the ones we use for our garden, and said, 'You come from the Jewish district, don't you? Clean it, Jew.' A blond, bull-necked Nazi put a top hat on my head. 'Very well, sir,' I said. I put the hat at a jaunty angle and swept the pavement, as ordered. People stopped and stared at me. I got annoyed and began to whistle a Jewish nationalist song:

As long as Jordan's water masses
Flow through the land of tears
Just as long we won't give up our aims
Our hopes and dreams—
Blood brothers . . .

"They looked at me, and I stopped whistling. Thank God, they had no idea what tune it was. Now I really went mad. I gripped the broom with both hands and, sweeping the pavement, I moved along, tap-dancing. Trudi, can you imagine? I expected to be shot at any moment. Then I heard roars of laughter from the crowd. I was so lucky, Walter, I was so lucky that the boys were not Germans. They were Austrian Nazis with a sense of humor. They let me go. But that wasn't all. Listen to this. I rushed along Kohlmarkt to tell you about it, when two German Nazis stopped me. 'Gentlemen,' I said, 'I've just come from your competitors.' 'What is your religion?' they demanded. 'Non-Aryan, believer in God,' I replied. They didn't understand, so they let me go. Who wants to educate people?"

Nobody spoke.

"Who wants to change Pepi?" I asked softly.

He gazed at his shoes, resting on the red Persian rug.

5

An epidemic was rife in Austria: denunciation. The true masters of the city were now the janitors. They denounced all the tenants with whom they had had rows in the past. Particularly Jews. Maids enjoyed a reign of terror, too. Over the years, these girls—who often had boyfriends in the Party—had heard all their employers' table talk and knew their political views inside out. There was now capital to be made out of this, or revenge to be taken, or envy to be assuaged.

The first real looting began. Jewish businesses and department stores were raided, mostly by youths. The synagogue in the Seitenstettengasse was occupied by the SS.

The humiliation of Jewish citizens continued. Their religious community association was closed down, its committee arrested. Aryan commissars were installed in every Jewish business. The owners could count themselves lucky if they didn't end up in a concentration camp or at the Viennese Hotel Metropole, now the Gestapo headquarters.

Austria's latent anti-Semitism came to the boil.

At Praterstern, the "Jewish district," as they called it, things were particularly bad. Men, women, and children knelt on the ground to scrub pavements. The crowd howled with pleasure. The so-called cleaning squad was ordered to wash a stenciled portrait of Schuschnigg off the pediment of a statue. Storm troopers dragged an aged Jewish workman and his wife through the delighted crowds. With tears rolling down her cheeks, she looked straight ahead, through her tormentors. She tried to pat her husband's hand.

"Work for Jews at last, work for Jews!" the mob howled. "We thank the Führer for finding work for the Jews!"

This is the truth about what happened, but I feel some reluctance to write it down. It is unfair to all those people who helped Jews. Many Austrians and some Germans, at tremendous risk to themselves, secretly did whatever was possible to help. I experienced great sympathy and many acts of kindness myself. So did my parents and friends. Austrians, with all their faults and weaknesses, were not really bad people. Nor were the Germans. But the mob now had the upper hand. The bitter, the envious, the unemployed. Worked up, ordered by their leaders to commit terrible crimes, they did as they were told. It took nerve to stand up to the Nazis. Not many heroes emerged from that diabolical period.

6

My trip paid off. I produced a collection with the models and materials I had bought in Paris. But my designs were less gay than those I had seen there. I used more veiling to hide women's eyes. To hide their sorrow. It couldn't possibly be a dressy season. People didn't go out in the evening anymore. Even non-Jewish customers were worried.

I decided to go for soft-brimmed sports hats in pastel felts, straw hats in dark or bright colors trimmed with velvet ribbons. One or two small flower toques and large picture hats. I had bought silk traced with a Persian design and turned out draped turbans with matching scarves.

I made enough money to support myself, to keep my parents, and to put a little aside. It was enough for me to keep my workroom going for now. I was fond of my girls. They had shown incredible loyalty. The feeling of being among friends was essential to me.

Outside, the climate was suffocating, but business was relatively good. Jewish customers and most other women still wanted my hats. But I wondered why they wanted hats at all.

I had two special customers: Gaby and Lilli. Gaby, Lilli, and Doris, my showroom lady, were great friends. They all shared a particular trait: greed—for position, money, and love.

Gaby didn't just walk into my salon, she strode in. Eyes like pools, dark, deep, pensive. Gaby carefully selected the men who were to be given the privilege of keeping her in luxury. For her, no nouveaux riches, vulgar, self-made men. Her men had to have been born into millions. And she had to love—or at least like—them. Gaby was, in short, a high-class courtesan.

She stood in front of the mirror, a little taller than average. She held herself straight: a classical beauty. She picked up my favorite beret, made of red roses, and put it on her dark, silky hair. Aristocratic looks, allure, pride—she had it all. (In the end, she married a handsome South American aristocrat, a multimillionaire, of course.)

"Too many veils for me," she said. "Even in Egypt, women are allowed to show their eyes. Let them see mine. Frau Trudi, Egypt is where you should go. Everybody's rich, and those who aren't are your servants. To protect you, they sleep on the floor outside your bedroom door. You want a glass of water, a drink, just clap your hands. And they have the finest stores. If you order clothes, they come to your home for fittings. Ready in forty-eight hours. Their shoes and bags made to order are a dream. And people throw unforgettable parties. And here is something you will like: the men call you *habibi*."

Lilli arrived. She wore a tight-fitting black velvet suit and stormed toward Gaby, arms outstretched to embrace her. A small, veiled straw beret sat on her flaming red hair.

"Darling Gaby, you look ravishing! A new dress! Look, Frau Trudi, look how clever she is. That deep, wide décolleté shows her beautiful straight back, her broad shoulders, and that divinely long neck. Gaby, I adore you. You have a new man! Admit!"

Gaby liked Lilli but didn't want to be seen with her. They always arranged to rendezvous at my salon. Lilli liked sex, she liked money, and, if she liked a man who could afford to keep her, she would live with him for a while. Sooner or later, she would move on to another man. For a month, a week, a night. She was a cocotte, without principle. Men wouldn't leave her alone.

"What's been happening?" Gaby asked her.

"He took possession of me with such force that afterward I suspected he had broken my ribs! There has to be a change! I will not pretend anymore that I love them so much." She crunched her lobster sandwich. "They need to know that they have to pay. I am entitled to be paid," she rasped, pacing. She smoked permanently. Her long, painted fingernails drummed the table.

"Cheated. I was cheated!" she shrieked. She took another puff of her cigarette. The fine veiling of her hat caught fire. She was in flames. We ran to her, dragged her to the floor, and pulled off the burning hat. Unhurt, except for her slightly singed hair, Lilli sat on the floor and cried. Her white skin had turned pink. Doris bent down and kissed her.

I said to her once, "Lilli, your way of living—don't you ever regret it?"

"Je ne regrette rien, jamais," she said in her Hungarian accent. Her small, reedlike body quivered.

(Lilli's breasts were famous. Round and firm. The nipples pink. Desirable. They saved her life, if you can call it a life. She ended up in a concentration camp. Because of her eroticism, and her beauty, and her delightful breasts, the Germans spared her from the gas chamber. They made her a camp whore. She survived. I heard she married an American soldier.)

Doris brought coffee and petits fours from Demel.

"Just what we need," Gaby said.

Lilli chose the draped silk turban with matching scarf. She wore the hat slightly tilted forward, added a short veil, and pushed all her hair inside. She looked exotic, Japanese. The blue-green of the Persian design was the exact color of her slanted mermaid eyes.

Gaby decided on the large picture hat in white, nearly

transparent straw. It had a small wreath of lilies of the valley around the crown.

Everybody kissed everybody good-bye. I sank back in my chair and sighed with relief.

7

Walter lived in an exquisite building at 7 Stubenring. The apartment was modern, luxurious, tasteful, designed by an American interior decorator.

Walter was informed that a German officer wished to buy his apartment for a nominal sum. He agreed, knowing that if he refused it would be requisitioned anyway. By offering this small amount, the officer wanted to make certain it was officially his. The deeds were to be signed within two days.

I suddenly remembered a particularly vicious anti-Nazi tract Walter had been reading. "Walter," I said. "That book is in your flat."

"Blast. I'll have to go and get it."

We went that same evening.

The front door to the building, dark brown mahogany, was heavily carved. The hall, lined with mahogany, was generously mirrored from floor to ceiling. I filched a red rose

from one of the flower arrangements and put it in my but-
tonhole.

The lift was silent. As were the porters, the tenants—even
their dogs. We went over to Walter's apartment in secret
to steal a book that belonged to Walter. We tried to creep
unnoticed into the flat that was still his. What a stupid situation! How childish we were! I wore a short, tight, black dress,
dark glasses, and short black gloves. My hair was covered by
a black beret that I wore at an angle. Walter's raincoat was
tightly belted, his collar turned up. The brim of his black hat
was pulled down over his face.

Entering his dimly lit French blue bedroom brought back
memories. It was there that I had stood at the windows, ner-
vously waiting for Walter to come home after Mira's funeral.
It was there that he had held me tight without saying a word,
and I realized that I had not lost him. The exquisite off-white
rug on the parquet floor made it feel as though you were
walking on a cloud.

I went into the library. The walls were lined with built-in
bookshelves. Leather-bound first editions of novels in German, English, and French. In the middle of this large room,
on a fine blue and red Persian rug, stood Walter's large desk.
Solid. A reflection of his reliability.

Between two windows, below a well-lit painting, was a
round table on which stood a silver candelabra with five
lights. I noticed that Walter had had the four dining chairs
reupholstered in blue raw silk. We used to have dinner here
by candlelight.

Walter called me into the white, mosaic-tiled bathroom. He had carefully wrapped up the book. He was taking his toothbrushes, his eau de cologne, and his carnation soap. Thick monogrammed towels and his dressing gown. A tube of toothpaste.

"Listen, darling," Walter said. "Now that we are here, we may as well take some other things, too."

The flat was the first thing that we had to say good-bye to. It was exciting, tiptoeing away. We took the two rugs.

For many years after that, Walter and I used to play a game:

"What hung over the French commode in my sitting room?"

"What was the lighting in the library?"

"What color were the shades on my bedside lamps?"

"What color were the curtains in the bedroom? In the bathroom? In the kitchen?"

"Did I have curtains in my hall?"

However long it had been, the answers always came quickly. We never forgot the homes we had loved so much.

One day, Walter asked, "What color were my pajamas the night you first stayed with me?"

"Shame on me," I said. "I can't remember."

8

We were afraid to go out. Officially, we were told nothing. There was no announcement in the newspaper or on the radio. We had so many questions. Who dared to ask them?

Suddenly, exit visas would be granted only if the applicant owed no taxes. Most of my customers disappeared, owing me money. Jewish bank accounts had been frozen. How would I pay my taxes? How would I get a visa?

The last house along Kohlmarkt on my side of the street was set well back, leaving a big expanse of corner pavement open. A flat roof extended over the pavement, protecting it from the rain. There, the Nazis put up a huge, black, velvet-covered table that held a white, life-size bust of Hitler.

They knew from experience that forcing just a few people to stand in line would spark a *perpetuum mobile* queue. This grew longer and longer; it dispersed at night and began again the following morning. As people passed the bust, they raised their right arms and shouted, "*Heil* Hitler!" Some kissed it. Some even went on their knees in front of it, thanking the Führer—without even knowing why.

* * *

There was a new newspaper: *Der Stürmer*. It was concerned only with "the Jewish question." It sought to prove to the gentile inhabitants of Austria what low, dirty, despicable criminals Jews were. They took photographs of Jews who had been imprisoned for weeks, half-starved and forbidden to shave; these photographs were accompanied by stories of their alleged crimes. The photographs and captions were then turned into posters and displayed all over Vienna. The first time I saw them, I felt sick. Gradually there were more and more of them. They seemed to get bigger and bigger until they were enormous and terrifying. The mass hysteria was so powerful that even I began to think, *Is it possible that we actually are such terrible people?*

A letter arrived from London, from Elli and Tina, two of my favorite customers. They were sisters-in-law whose husbands had many business connections in England. The week before the occupation of Austria, they had gone to London, supposedly on holiday.

I hadn't been in touch with them; I didn't even know that they had left. Now they wanted to help me escape. They were related to the owners of a large chain of department stores in Holland called Bijenkorf. They had mentioned me to them, and Bijenkorf had offered to employ me as a hat designer and head of millinery in its Rotterdam store. The sisters told me that all I had to do was apply for the job, sending a short CV and a recent photograph.

I had never answered a letter so quickly in my life, and almost by return a contract arrived from Bijenkorf. Enclosed was a letter to the Dutch border authorities. A miracle had happened. I had an entry permit to Holland and a first-class job. But what about Walter?

"Darling, why don't you write to your uncle in London?" Walter had told me about this man, who had been naturalized for forty years and was married to an Englishwoman. "I'm sure he will send you a guarantee, or a letter of invitation, and you'll get a visa for England. Once we're out of here, we'll find a way to be together."

"I can't write to him—I only met him once, and that was twenty years ago. He's a stranger; he won't help us."

"You have to try, Walter! Doing nothing will get nothing."

No reply. I realized it was useless to argue.

Things grew more and more grave. We still heard the "cleaning squad" stories. But more often now we heard of friends and acquaintances being taken from their homes, leaving their families with heartache, terror, suicide.

One morning, the bridge over the Danube connecting Franz Josef Quay with Leopoldstadt was suddenly closed at both ends. Halfway across the bridge stood a huge, open cattle truck. People trapped on the bridge were sorted into Jews and non-Jews. The non-Jews were allowed to leave. Jews were thrown into the van. Who knows how many arrived at their destination with broken bones? Who knows how many arrived at all?

9

Pepi came to see me. He was very excited. A letter from the Millers' rich American aunt had come out of the blue—they had not written to her to ask for help. She would guarantee the whole family. They were told to go to the American consulate to collect their visas.

"Pepi, how wonderful! I'm so happy for you."

"Yes—but the snag is that my parents were born in Czechoslovakia."

To limit immigration, the United States had assigned a quota to each country. The size of the quota depended on the population of that country. You were bound to the quota of the country of your birth, and US visas were issued according to your quota number.

"The quota for Czechoslovakia is exhausted. One year's waiting list."

I had never seen Pepi look so desperate.

"Austrian quota numbers are easily available, and as all of us children were born in Vienna, we will probably be able to leave very soon."

"What will you do, Pepi?"

"If all else fails, I'll stay behind."

"You can't do that. You must leave with the others."

"Will has an idea. We could try to get our parents to

South America where they will be safe; they can wait there until they are allowed to enter the US. Trudi, God will help us. Listen, I have some more news for you, good news."

He had asked his aunt to extend her guarantee to include Walter and me.

Olli Loewinger came to see me, with her daughter and a young American. Mother was charming, but I had never liked the daughter, Sarah, who was plain and sulky. The American boy was lovely. Squat, open, friendly face, crew cut. Always laughing.

"This is Nat," Olli said. "Sarah and Nat are engaged. I came to say good-bye—we're going to America."

"How lucky you are," I said. "Congratulations."

"You know how they met?" Olli said. "It was an act of God. Sarah was knocked down by a bicycle at the very moment that Nat was passing on his motorbike. It's a miracle. He put her on his pillion and brought her home. He has never left her since."

Nat was a student, and in with the staff at the American consulate. Olli and her daughter already had American visas and quota numbers. Their money and jewelry would go in the diplomatic bag.

"Nat, we have a guarantee from an American relative, which I hope will arrive soon. What's the situation with the quota?" I asked.

"Can you and Walter meet me tomorrow at the consulate at three p.m.?"

"We'll do anything, if you can help us."

"I will. Don't worry."

Our quota numbers were three and four.

PART THREE

A Fashion Show

(Paris, 1935)

1

I had a friend called Mitzi, who also owned a hat salon in Vienna. Within two weeks of the German occupation of Austria, busy Mitzi had found a young man. Jewish. Born in England. British passport. Poor. In need of money to buy new clothes, new teeth, and a ticket to England.

They married. Tomorrow, Mitzi would step onto English soil, an English lady. There was no one like Mitzi.

I remember when she used to go regularly to the Paris shows, and the time she invited me to join her . . .

It was 1935 when we took the express train to Paris, a twenty-four-hour journey. We settled ourselves in upholstered corner seats. Doors were slammed, porters stood back. The whistle shrieked, the engine blew white steam, the train rattled, shook, and began to move.

How exciting, I thought. *I'll meet interesting people. Broaden my horizons.*

We ate our homemade sandwiches, drank coffee from

our flasks. The train was packed; we had to sit up straight. Eventually, Mitzi fell asleep. I looked at her blond hair, her china complexion. She was small and slim; her broad shoulders and short neck made her look square. I had accepted her invitation to Paris because I knew she was businesslike and shrewd. I would learn a lot.

Mitzi was single, and man-mad. The boyfriend, the fiancé, the *husband* of her very best friend: Mitzi tried hard—without subtlety, and without success.

The restaurant car attendant woke her, ringing his bell. "First service for breakfast! Ladies and gentlemen, take your seats!"

Mitzi rushed to the dining car, took a table with window seats. A French waiter appeared, wearing a white linen jacket, white napkin over his arm. He had dark eyes, liked the girls. We ate eggs fried in butter, served sizzling hot in the flat aluminum pans in which they had been cooked. The bread rolls were crisp and hot. Coffee was served with boiling milk.

Our hotel was small, old-fashioned but not expensive. We had a pleasant room. Mitzi annexed the better-positioned bed, then made for the wardrobe, appropriating four of the six hangers.

Mitzi explained how things worked. "The Paris houses know that small firms like ours can't afford a lot. But we have to stick to their rules. They know we will copy everything we can remember, and they can't do anything about that. We just have to try to get away with as much as we can. Watch me— I'll show you how to copy without their noticing. When you are holding the model hat, you can measure. Use the length of your thumb, your middle finger and your little finger. Use the palm of your hand and the length from your wrist to the end of your middle finger. Color, shape, and trimming you have to memorize, and then apply the measurements you have taken."

I was amazed, and a little uneasy.

In the dining room at breakfast, Mitzi got the best table and took the best seat. She snatched the brownest, crispest roll and tasted everything on my plate, offering nothing from her own. *Now I know why she's never had a man,* I thought. Her eyes, round, like large marbles, were light blue. Left-right, left-right, they never missed a thing.

I walked through Paris in a dream. Rue de la Paix, avenue Foch, Champs-Elysées: luxury at its best, its most international. The world's most elegant hotels. Huge lobbies were filled with comfortable armchairs, soft sofas, mirrored walls, thick carpets. Flower arrangements as tall as trees. The commissionaire was tall, gold-braided, an exiled Russian aristocrat, one of many. The Russians were tour guides, waiters, porters, taxi drivers, and were good-looking and polite. They gave comfort with humility, not servility. They were still aristocrats.

Paris in 1935 was incredible. Charming people, beautiful buildings, wide boulevards. We sat outside one of the cafés lining the Champs-Elysées. Five years later, Hitler would ride along there in triumph, right through the Arc de Triomphe.

Shops were sparkling glass and metal outside, mirrored

walls within, reflecting the colors of that season. Girls with swinging hair, swinging handbags and hips, wear jangling bracelets and ropes of pearls and many rings. They are slender and well-coiffed, have clear, petal-smooth complexions, wear tiny hats, veils, camellias in buttonholes.

"When I'm in my late thirties, I want to live in Paris," Mitzi said. "No one here wonders about your age. They don't care."

Suddenly I see my reflection in a shopwindow: walking shoes, practical coat, sports hat. I feel absurd and want to go home.

To get the feel of the season's modes, we had to see at least one show that included dresses as well as hats. We make our way to a prestigious model house.

There is a mystique about these places. Carpeted stairs, mirrored walls, flowers everywhere: on the marble-topped commode, on the desk, on the stairs, upstairs, everywhere. Their reflection in the mirrors competes with that of the numerous crystal chandeliers.

"You have your invitation, mademoiselle?" The directrice stands in front of me: arrogant, condescending, piercing tones. A small woman with a small head, small gray eyes, and small feet. A tall, moustached gentleman stands behind her. He has a large mouth and huge teeth. Mitzi explains our credentials, gives our names, our addresses, the names of our salons in Vienna. She commits us to buy. I can see that they are not satisfied. They are still suspicious. But we will be allowed to see the show.

Crowding the hall, lining the stairs, peering out of the

showroom is an army of employees bursting with pride and importance and wearing superior smiles. They are watching us.

The large showroom has a gray carpet. There are enormous gilt-framed mirrors and small, silver-gray moiré-covered chairs in rows. The first row is occupied by bejeweled ladies. Some young, mink-coated; some old, mink-coated; fat or slim, beautiful or plain, mink-coated. The really chic women wear tweed suits, a little gold jewelry, sables.

Mitzi recognizes a famous actor but can't remember his name. "Look," she whispers. "He has a cowboy's face. His nose has been smashed—several times. He seems educated and gentle. The contrast drives women wild. He is so sexy!"

We take our seats. The saleslady places a program and a pencil in our laps. "For marking the names of the hats we like," Mitzi whispers. "Don't be tempted to sketch, or we'll be blacklisted."

The showroom is crowded. Glasses of champagne are offered, tension mounts, the show begins. I hardly dare breathe.

Mannequin after mannequin glides through, passes us, turns around, shows clothes and hats quickly from every angle. Spring is to be a flower season. A toque made entirely of violets. Large, floppy hats of black horsehair braid, the crows covered in white cabbage roses. A large, soft beret of roses in all shades of pink and red. The bride wears a skullcap of white camellias, a white camellia bracelet on her left wrist. The applause is tremendous.

We have seen almost a hundred hats. I can remember twenty.

"Look behind you! Your saleslady is waiting," Mitzi whispers. "She appeared like the secret police."

I am convinced that they were watching us through little holes in the ceiling.

We order two model hats and say good-bye. *"Merci, madame." "Merci, mademoiselles." "Bon voyage." "Au revoir." "Merci beaucoup."* The process of good-byes is repeated on the ground floor. *"Bonjour, madame." "Merci beaucoup." "Au revoir."*

We are on the pavement. There is no time to draw breath. We rush to the nearest bistro, find a corner table, and order ham sandwiches. They arrive and are half a yard long. I feel exhausted; my mouth is dry. A small brandy, a small Perrier, my sketchbook, my pencil. I write a description of each hat I can remember. Then I sketch them. I calculate the size of each brim, the depth and width of each crown. Mitzi's tips have helped. Then we go to the outskirts of Paris, to the poorer suburbs, where the wholesalers are. We choose straw, velvet, silk, flowers, feathers, pins.

On our way to the railway station to catch our train back to Vienna, we have to go through a revolving door. Mitzi makes me go first—she wants me to push. But before I can enter my section, she has flitted in herself. I have to go in second, and push again.

She can't understand why I can't stop laughing.

PART FOUR

The Glass Roof

(Vienna, 1938)

1

The doorbell rang twice in quick succession. It was Mitzi.

She looked pretty. There was more shine and depth in her eyes. Her blond hair was lighter; she held her head higher, which made her neck seem longer. Success was written all over her.

"Come in, Mitzi. Come on through."

Her eyes darted left-right, left-right, registering everything in my sitting room.

We sat by the window, drinking coffee. Sun, blue sky. Peace. That was a lifetime ago.

"What will you do in London?" I asked. "Do you have any contacts?"

"Yes, quite a few. Customers of mine. Hat manufacturers and wholesalers. I've already been in touch—they seem eager to help. What about you and Walter?"

I told her about my job offer in Rotterdam. About the possibility of the United States. I told her that Walter was bitter and frustrated. And that I was unhappy and worried that I hadn't yet found anything for him. Suddenly, I had an idea. I asked Mitzi to help.

She saved my life, Walter's life, and the lives of our families.

She sent me three letters from English hat manufacturers. They said that they were very interested in seeing my collection of model hats. They were keen to buy. Armed with these letters, I visited the *Handelskammer*, the Board of Trade.

I told them I needed permission to travel abroad on business. They thought I was joking.

"Fräulein, don't you know that we're not Austria anymore? We're Germany now, and Germany is boycotted. We can't sell abroad."

"*I* can," I said quietly. "May I show you these?" I gave them the letters Mitzi had sent me. I translated them. They shook their heads, shrugged, and instructed a clerk to take me to see the head of the department.

His office didn't seem to fit with the otherwise modern style of the *Handelskammer*. It was old-fashioned, solid, simple. The man behind the desk was huge. Quite old. He looked at me over his round, metal-rimmed spectacles, pointed to a chair, told me to sit, and asked the clerk to wait outside. He carried on reading the papers he had been reading when I came in. The only sound in the room was the ticking of an enormous wooden clock hanging on the wall.

He looked up. "What can I do for you, young lady?" His accent was upper-class Austrian.

I told him that I needed permission from the *Handelskammer* to go on a business trip to England. I knew all about the boycott, but I felt certain I could do business. I explained that most of my customers had left Austria, and I needed to replace the lost turnover. For a while he sat quite still. His fat fingers stroked his balding head, ruffling his sparse, gingery gray hair. His muddy carp's eyes, old and wise, looked straight ahead. Five minutes, ten minutes. Why was he taking such a long time? It was yes or no. The ticking of the clock seemed to get louder. Then he lifted his heavy body off his creaking chair, clasped his hands behind his back, walked to the window and stared outside. Eternity.

"What makes you so sure you can sell?" He turned to me. "Did you export before?"

"Very little," I said. "But I know that I can now."

"Why should you think that? Let me tell you that there are firms who, before the boycott, did thousands of pounds' worth of business with England, and they can do nothing now. What makes you think you are any different?"

"These, sir." I put my letters on his desk.

I was lucky. The man spoke English, and he was very proud to be able to read them.

"Well, young lady," he said, with a twitch of a smile. "Let's see how many hats we used to export before the *Anschluss.*"

He picked up the telephone and asked for these figures. *Oh, God, please let it be a lot!* I bit my nails. He noticed. The twitch at the corner of his mouth reappeared. Suddenly, the old clock gathered its forces, took a deep breath, screeched, rattled, and announced the three-quarter hour with three thunderous strokes. The telephone rang.

"Yes," he said. "Is this the figure for the last year? Thank you. Yes, that will be all."

He looked at my letters again.

"Frau Miller. *Frau*?" A gallant, surprised look at me. "Frau Miller, the export figures for hats last year were excellent. But that doesn't mean I can give you a *Handelskammer* permission to go to England. It is not enough. I want you to know that if I do let you go, it is against the instructions I have been given, and I am taking a great risk. Tell me, where exactly do you want to go?"

"I want to go to London with my collection, where I hope to get good orders. On my way back, I would like to stop for a few days in Paris to see the new hat shows. And from there to Holland, where I hope to get more orders."

"That sounds rather a big undertaking."

"No, sir, I've done it before."

"All right," he said. "In the next few days, you will receive our permit and letters to the consulates of the countries you mentioned. I have confidence in you. You see, many people would take this opportunity and never return." He looked straight into my eyes. "Good luck, young lady," he said, and turned away.

I was stunned.

"Don't forget what I told you," he said.

"No, sir, I won't. Thank you."

I floated through the door, past the young clerk, into the street on the way to No. 11, straight into Walter's arms.

"That's wonderful. Wonderful. Darling, you're safe!" His

eyes were larger, bluer. "I'm so proud of you. How did you do it?"

"I don't know. I was just lucky. He advised me not to come back . . ."

There was one hurdle left.

Next morning, I was at the tax office as the doors opened. I went straight to the first floor to see my tax man. I liked and trusted him. I told him about the business trip I intended to take and explained why I could not possibly pay my income tax right then. He understood the circumstances, but he couldn't help me.

"You need to speak to the man in charge of exit visas. I'll take you over there."

I had to wait to be called in. I had to repeat my story and show him my letters. He was small and tight-faced, withdrawn, unfriendly, bad-tempered.

"Fräulein," the man said, "the law is the law. And the law says that an exit permit cannot be granted unless all taxes are paid in full. You haven't paid them, have you? So, you cannot have an exit permit. Right?" He had nasty little bird's eyes.

I collected myself, looked down, and said in the smallest, softest voice I could muster, "Please, sir. Help me."

He gave a disagreeable smile.

I explained that, through circumstances beyond my control, I was penniless. That I would be able to pay my taxes only if I were permitted to make this trip and earn some money. My tax man and the visa man exchanged glances.

"Well," said the visa man. "You have been warmly recommended. In the opinion of the tax office, you can be trusted. So I will take it upon myself to make an exception." He took a form from his desk, signed it, and gave it to my savior from the tax office. Then he turned to me and said, "You will be given this form after it has been stamped. Now you have your exit permit. I hope that you will earn a lot of money. You owe us a lot of money. Good-bye."

My friend from the tax office pulled me into an empty office and said, "Quick, before he changes his mind. Wait here."

He was back in minutes and handed me the stamped form, a big grin on his face. It was the most important piece of paper I had ever held in my hands.

"Good luck to you," he said. His face was serious. "Frau Miller, in case you intend not to return to Austria, I want you to think before you decide. Look"—he turned over his lapel and showed me his swastika pin—"I have been a member of the Party for a long time. Our arrangement with the Germans is as follows: they come in to establish a National Socialist state. Having done so, they will leave again. Austria will be run by us. By Austrians. We will have our own version of National Socialism. I want you to know that Jewish people like yourself will not be affected. You, your parents, and your grandparents were born in this country. You are Austrians and have nothing to fear."

I tried to hide my tears and turned to the window. A group of girls marched by. Sharp steps, one-two. Heads high, one-two. Hair short, practical. Uniforms practical. White knee socks. *Heil* Hitler.

"Look at them," he said. "They call themselves women."

The rest was easy. With the letters from the *Handelskammer*, I had only to gather the English and French visas. I had the letter from Bijenkorf to the Dutch border authorities requesting permission for my entry into Holland. The Czech visa was easily added. The greatest task still lay ahead. I had to find a way to get a visa for Walter.

2

Walter sits at the window, despair in his eyes.

"Darling, don't be upset. Please don't. It's not your fault. You have had no opportunity to get a visa. I only got the chance because of my business. What does it matter who gets us out of this mess, as long as we get out? I have plans. I'm sure one of them will work. Don't destroy my hopes. Don't make me unhappy. I need all the strength I can get. Help me. Please."

He holds my hand and strokes it.

All my life, I had tried to achieve things with kindness, with love and reason. But they are not helping now. I change tack.

"Why don't you write to your uncle?"

His face tightens.

"You know that it's your only option. Why don't you try it? You take the line of least resistance. Anybody can do that. And you won't even let *me* write to him. Do you remember when the Nazis marched into Kohlmarkt and I wanted to leave straightaway? Do you remember what you said? You said, 'What we fear will come later.' Walter, later is *now*."

When I go to bed, there is a note on my pillow with his uncle's name and address.

The window is open. A breeze parts the drawn curtains slightly. A small beam of light appears on the ceiling. It comes and goes. Walter sleeps beside me.

Tomorrow I will write the letter. If Walter can't leave, I won't. And if I don't leave, my parents can't.

I close my eyes. Long ago, a feather and a sequin was a hat.

12 May 1938

Dear Uncle Paul,

May I call you that? In a few days, Walter and I will be married.

I assume that you know the trouble we are in. The whole world knows. Can you help? Will you? It is a matter of life and death.

I already have a visa for the United Kingdom. It is for Walter that I ask your help.

Please send him an invitation, or a letter of guarantee.
With this, he will be able to gain entry to England. We will be
grateful. This is meant sincerely. You see, if Walter can't get
out of here, I will stay with him.

We will be no burden to you, financially or otherwise. I am
a hat designer, and my firm is quite well-known in England. It
should not be difficult for me to get a job as a designer. I have
some money and jewelry. That will enable us to get a place to
live, to buy time until we find a way of earning our living.

Walter said that you will not help him because you hardly
know him. I cannot believe that. Strangers from all over the
world are helping to save the lives of people like us. And Wal-
ter is your nephew. Uncle, please, we are running out of time.

I very much hope that I will be able to meet you and will be
in a position to thank you personally for your kindness.
Yours,
Trudi Miller

In the middle of the night, I woke up and knew what to do.

In the millinery trade, hats are shaped on wooden blocks,
and as fashion changes so quickly, these blocks, which are
expensive, can be used for only a season. A man in the trade,
a Mr. Kaltenbrunner, had found a way to manufacture a similar product for a quarter of the price.

I went to Mr. Kaltenbrunner to talk to him about his
invention. I came to an arrangement with him and took out
a patent in my name.

There was huge unemployment at that time in England. The British vice-consul's wife was one of my clients, and I thought she might be able to help. I told her about the patent I had taken out and suggested that the new kind of hat block might help to create work in her country.

"Do you think that your husband could put in a word?" I asked. "I would be so grateful. I'm sure he will realize what this means to us. If it weren't so important, I wouldn't dream of asking."

Next morning, she returned in triumph with her husband's card. He had written a note on the back suggesting that he would greatly appreciate the help of the consulate in this matter.

I hurried over to the British consulate with the note. I explained to the young Englishwoman behind the desk why I had come, and wondered if someone could help me. The whole time I was speaking, she looked past me. I handed her the vice-consul's card. She took it. Without looking at it, she tore it up, dropped it into the wastepaper basket, turned around, and walked away.

Walter, my darling. You didn't know how desperate I was. Maybe this was God's punishment for my having made you suffer. Remember when I made you jealous? I never wanted to upset you.

Francesco was an irresistible Italian aristocrat. Count Francesco Scocchera di Santa Vittoria.

I met him in Vienna during those confused days and weeks before the German occupation of my country. Vienna was preparing for spring. Green shutters on white villas were painted greener. Black railings had their pointed gilt tops regilded. At the coffeehouses, newly white-painted chairs and tables were hopefully put outside. Waiters in white linen jackets carried white napkins over their arms. They welcomed the sun and invited customers to be the first ones to sit outside.

The city looked crisp and polished, full of goodwill and expectation. Full of romance. Even strangers greeted each other with a big smile and a bright, "Good morning."

Walter had a business meeting with Francesco's cousin, Paolo. A dark-eyed, dark-haired, good-looking Italian. He had brought Francesco along, and Walter telephoned me to invite me to join them. Lunch was at the Three Hussars, the "in" restaurant at the time. In the dining room there was just enough room for one round table on each side. The white, starched tablecloths and napkins looked striking against the red walls.

Slender, of medium height, Francesco had the face of an aesthete. Light blond hair, deep-set olive green eyes. He hid an incisive brain behind an air of mild bafflement.

Later, Walter asked, "What do you think of him?"

"He's superb," I said. "I have never met anyone like him. Have you?"

No reply. I carried on teasing him. "Gertrud, Contessa Scocchera di Santa Vittoria."

"Oh, stop it!" he thundered, and blew out of the room.

That evening, we all went to a nightclub.

Francesco was a bachelor of thirty-four. A lawyer and architect, he owned the largest building firm in Milan. I couldn't resist his flattery. Francesco intoxicated me with words. I had never met a man like him—a count. I couldn't escape the soft net blown around me. The open attention. The compliments.

We were dancing. Francesco whispered in my ear: "I'm lucky to have found you."

Catastrophe! I sprained my ankle, and the dancing had to stop. Next morning, a bouquet arrived—thirty-six red roses held by white orchids. A card: "I hope your ankle is better. Are you able and willing to meet me? Francesco."

He had hired a fiaker, an open horse-drawn carriage.

"Where would you like to go, and what would you like to see?" I asked.

"You!" he replied.

I avoided his eyes, wanting neither to hurt nor encourage him.

"Show me what you like best," he said. "I'm sure I'll like it, too."

"Francesco, I love all of it—and I love Walter."

We took a slow ride to the Prater, the lovely old-fashioned park I had visited with Walter—restaurants, beer gardens, an amusement park, the Ferris wheel. People walked in the woods. Youngsters rode horses, laughing and calling to each other. Birds chirped. The scent of the new green.

"Auf Wiedersehen, gnädige Frau, mein Herr," said the fiaker, doffing his round, flat hat.

We were back at my apartment. I asked Francesco to have coffee with me.

He told me that Mussolini's dictatorship had become unbearable and he had decided to leave Italy. He had spirited large amounts of money out of Italy to Switzerland. If his transactions were discovered, he would be in serious trouble.

"Anything could happen," he said. "Trudi, stretch your imagination to the limit."

"But Francesco . . ."

"Don't say any more. I want to marry you."

"Francesco, I love Walter."

"We will talk about love when I come back. Which will be soon."

He stood on top of the steps of his wagon-lit, talking to me as I stood on the platform. He held my hands. As the train began to move, he tightened his grip. He tried to pull me up to him. It was so unexpected, I lost my balance. Two porters, who had been watching, helped me off the already moving train. It was heading nonstop to Milan.

I saw Francesco's outstretched arms and troubled face receding.

There was no word for two weeks. Returning home one day, I was told of a telephone call from Milan. A lady with an Italian accent had tried to contact me urgently. She promised to telephone again.

A week later, thirty-six red roses arrived. I wrote, sent a telegram. No reply. Telephone calls went unanswered.

The Germans came. Walter and I married. There was no news of Francesco. I didn't know where he was. I had no new address to give him.

I wish he hadn't said, "Trudi, stretch your imagination to the limit."

My friend Doris, who worked in my showroom, was most upset.

"How can you, Trudi? How can you say no? A name like his. Imagine! You would be the Contessa Scocchera di Santa Vittoria. Any girl would marry him. Just for the name!"

Doris had affairs with men—and women. Money didn't come into it. Doris was a sucker for love. Her father was a professor, her mother a doctor. They were baptized Jews. Both parents died of cancer. Poor Doris was permanently terrified. She examined her body constantly. Maybe this terror explained the wild life she led.

I had known her since childhood, running around Vienna, joyous. Even as a child, her body was heavy, but her legs and arms were slim. She was beautiful, intelligent, and witty, a success with everyone. Once I asked her, "Who in this world do you love the most?" The answer came quickly, without hesitation: "My cousin Violet." For years, Doris had an affair with Violet's husband.

I last saw her when she came to visit us one evening at home. She wore a red velvet cape, its hood resting against her black hair. Walter opened the door. She stood still, smiling at him, showing her white teeth and her pink gums. She took no notice of me all evening.

Soon afterward, she married a man ten years her junior. With the guarantee of Violet's husband, they managed to go to America.

Doris died of cancer.

3

"Trudi, I'm going out," called Walter through the workroom door. He stood in the hall, hand on the doorknob, eager to leave.

"Do you have to? You know how I worry."

"I can't sit at home all the time," he said irritably. "I have to go out sometimes. And I need to see what's happening with my car."

A few weeks ago, he had taken it to the garage to be serviced.

"I want to see what they've done to it," he said. "I'll be home for lunch."

Doris is in the showroom, looking after customers. I don't want to see anyone. I go to the kitchen to prepare some cold food. Poor Walter. He seems numbed. I lay the table, add some flowers, and open the window to let the sun come in. Walter used to be strong, someone to lean on. Now his pride is hurt. He feels useless.

There is a mechanical whir from the cuckoo clock. Out pops the red and green painted bird. "Cuckoo!" I used to love it. Today, its beady black eyes and its frozen expression mock me. When I was little, my parents took me on a mountain holiday; I fell in love with the clock, and they bought it for me. Now, in its ridiculous voice, the cuckoo tells me that it is one o'clock. The telephone rings. I race to answer it. It is a business call.

Usually we have lunch at twelve thirty. Maybe he has been held up at the garage. One thirty. Walter is reliable. If he is running late, he telephones. Maybe the telephone is out of order? I lift the receiver and hear the dial tone. Maybe the telephone at the garage is out of order? Of course it isn't. Something has happened to him. I am frantic.

I don't know the name of the garage. There is nothing I can do but wait. Be calm. I go to my sitting room, stand at the window, and look down at Kohlmarkt. I can see nearly the whole street.

"Refugees from Nazi Oppression." That is what they called the German Jews who came to Austria seeking shelter. What a terrible description. I didn't understand what it meant. I didn't know that one day, I would be one. It is two o'clock.

Walter, please come home. Together we will be Refugees from Nazi Oppression. The door opens; someone comes in; I don't turn around.

Steffi says, "Madame, what's happened?" She turns me to face her. "Good God, madame, what's happened?"

By now, I am shaking all over. I sit down on the floor. She sits down next to me, puts her arm around me. She strokes my head, kisses my hands. I am crying. She asks no questions. She puts me to bed. I can't stop crying. She brings me a cup of coffee. I am calmer.

"Steffi, I can't ring the hospitals to find out if there has been an accident. I can't ring the police. I can't do anything in case they *don't* have him. It would draw attention to him. It could be very dangerous."

Steffi brings a large glass of brandy. I drink all of it and fall asleep.

Someone kisses me. I wake up. Walter smiles through tears. We gaze at each other. We embrace. We laugh. I jump out of bed.

"Hungry?"

He nods. I take his hand, and we run into the kitchen. We are ravenous.

Walter was on his way home when three Brownshirts took him to the former headquarters of the Vaterländische Front. The building had been repaired, and now they needed cleaning squads.

"They ordered me to scrub floors," Walter said, "polish floors, clean shelves and furniture. People were cleaning carpets, windows, and lavatories. Trudi, you know how I am. I did a perfect job. Then one of the young Nazis said, 'The old man has worked well. He can go home.' I looked around me for the old man. 'I mean you,' he said, pointing at me. I said, 'Thank you,' put on my coat, went downstairs, and crossed the street. I came home to you. I never thought that a bit of gray at the temples made you an old man. Does it?"

"I'll have to think about that, darling. Maybe those boys are right. Maybe you're too old for me."

He shook me, kissed me.

The incident had worked wonders. Walter was his old self again.

"What happened to your car?"

"It's gone."

"What do you mean? Gone where?"

"They stole it, Trudi. They stole my beautiful car. There's nothing I can do about it."

"Walter, I don't understand."

"Well, my dear, when I asked Sepp if my car was ready, he said, 'What car?' 'My car, my large, black, open-topped Fiat,' I said. 'I don't know anything about your car. Who are you?' 'You know very well who I am.' 'Josef,' he called to his pal, 'do you know this fellow? His car?' They laughed. 'I have never seen you before, and I never want to see you again, understand?' 'I do, Sepp. I do understand.' I walked away. You know what happened next. Enough for one day, darling.

Enough. They took my beautiful flat. Today, they took my beautiful car. They made me scrub floors. What next?"

"This." I kiss him.

My hand slips inside his shirt. I feel the hair on his chest.

Next day, Walter says, "Look at this." He hands me a letter. I don't look at it; I look at his face. His expression is serious.

"I don't want to read it. Tell me what it is."

"Just read it." He is smiling now.

The letter is from Uncle Paul. The Home Office in London has granted Walter a three-month visa. The British consulate in Vienna will let him know when it is ready for collection.

We dance, we make plans. We wouldn't change places with anyone in the world. We decide to celebrate, to take a chance. We're crazy. For the first time in a long time, we dress up. He watches me pull my black linen frock over my head and tug at it. I step into my purple sandals, get my large, purple linen bag. Walter calls a taxi. We have everything we need for our escape. We are taking a risk. Is youth an excuse for insanity?

We are in a small, intimate restaurant in a quiet, non-Jewish district. The waiter, green waistcoat with wide, white shirtsleeves, a big, striped apron, shows us to our table. Walter has asked if we can sit in a corner of the garden, under an apple tree. On my left is a small, neglected rose tree. One perfect rose, the colors of crevettes. There is a Hungarian violinist. He plays well, goes from table to table. He asks us to choose a song:

Mei muaterl war a Wienerin
Drum hab ich Wien so gern
My mother was Viennese
That's why I love Vienna

More people arrive. Which ones are the Nazis? Will they know we are Jews? I don't want to think about it. Tonight, we will go wild. I drink wine, eat grilled veal. Walter orders a steak, cooked over charcoal.

"I used to love barbecues when I was a boy scout. We would cook our sausages over an open fire." His hand feels for my leg under the starched tablecloth.

Apple blossoms fall into our hair, our laps, our food.

A blond child wanders from table to table, looks at me shyly. I pull a lock of my hair across my eyes, then slowly lower it. He runs away. He is about three or four, wearing tiny shorts and a blue pullover. Why isn't he in bed? I look around. We don't need to be afraid. These people are drinking, enjoying themselves. They don't care about anything.

"Walter, turn around. There is a little white house up on the hill—tell me what it says to you."

He looks, turns back to me, and smiles. "Never mind what it says to *me*," he says. "I'll tell you what it says to *you*."

"So?"

"You think that the people living behind the white curtains don't have to run."

I kiss him. I don't care who sees it. Damn them.

"There's a moon coming up," says Walter. The atmosphere between us is electric. His eyes are beautiful.

It was his idea to order a whole bottle of wine. I fall asleep if I drink more than a glass. He has to take me home and put me to bed.

Night and morning merge. I wake up with a headache.

4

"Who is he?" Walter asked.

"Who?"

"You know perfectly well who. The good-looking young man you talked to at Graben."

"Oh, you mean Gustl! Gustl Waud. I've known him for years. He was a friend of Pepi's."

"Was?"

"Pepi didn't want him around anymore after we were married. He was after me. He's like that. Always after someone else's girl."

"So why did you talk to him for so long?"

"We were talking about old times. About American quota numbers. He's waiting for his. He was jealous of our connection at the consulate. Anyway, how do you know how long

I spent talking to him? You weren't watching me the whole time, were you? Are you jealous? Good God! Jealous of Gustl Waud!" I laughed.

"Why not? He's your type."

"Oh, Walter, you're lovely when you're jealous." Still laughing, I ran into the kitchen.

"Miss," said the clerk at the American consulate, looking at me with bullet gray eyes set in a square face. "We are overrun with people like you. They all want to know what has happened to their visas. Our New York office is swamped with inquiries. You just have to be patient."

Patient? When our lives are at stake?

I couldn't sleep. Why hadn't we heard from the British consulate either? Surely Walter's visa should have arrived by now? My divorce from Pepi—I couldn't leave Austria until that came through. To get a divorce from abroad would be extremely difficult. It could take ages. And the money for my parents? I would have to leave them enough for at least six months. And when—and how—would I get them out?

I touched Walter's hand. He was asleep. I always had to reassure myself that he was there. Funny that Walter should be jealous of Gustl. One of the few people I disliked. Selfish. Mean. Conceited. Manufacturing soft drinks had made him a rich man. I heard the chime of the clock in the sitting room. It was three a.m. Walter rolled over to me.

"Why aren't you asleep, darling? Something wrong?" A big yawn. He snuggled closer.

"I'm counting my worries."

He turned the light on. A glow spread over his face. It looked so young. To hell with my worries. To hell with money, visas, and divorces. To hell with everything, as long as I had him.

"What are the worries?"

"Nothing, darling, nothing. I'll tell you tomorrow. Come closer."

When we woke up, Walter didn't say, "Good morning. Did you sleep well?" He said, "What worries?"

I told him. And I told him more about what Gustl had told me. "You know, Walter, he is clever. The moment the Germans set their first boot on Austrian soil, he withdrew a huge amount of money from the bank. He used some of it to buy diamonds, and he keeps them in a hidden safe with the rest of the cash."

Two days later, the telephone rang. "Trudi, you have to help me!" shouted Gustl. "My quota number hasn't arrived yet. I have enemies, Trudi. I can't sleep. If the doorbell rings, I pretend to be out. Help me, please. They are coming for me. I'm a nervous wreck. Talk to that man who helped you. Maybe he will do the same for me. I'm willing to pay for it. Whatever he wants, as long as I can get away quickly. Can you talk to him?"

"I'll try," I said, knowing full well that my connection was already back in America. "Meet me tomorrow at Demel. Two o'clock."

"What did he want?" Walter asked.

"He's in trouble. He wants me to help him."

"I bet."

"Walter, I have to."

"Well, Trudi?" Gustl's voice was shaking. The hand holding his cigarette was shaking.

"He's agreed," I said. "But he wants a lot of money."

"That's all right. Never mind the money. It means my life."

"He promised to put your application at the top of the pile."

I was taking a gamble, but nothing would be lost if the papers didn't arrive soon. If they did, it would seem like my doing.

Two days later, a jubilant Gustl telephoned. "The letter from the consulate has arrived! I'm safe—I'm leaving as soon as possible."

A miracle, another miracle, I thought. *God, dear God, thank you.* I wondered whether Gustl would pay me. He did. At once. He didn't say thank you. I didn't care. I had asked for the exact sum my parents would need for the next six months. They would be financially secure.

I didn't feel guilty.

5

I was in Hiess, the luxury department store downstairs from my apartment, buying a present for my mother. The window displays were beautiful. A salesman greeted me; I had often seen him in Demel. Dark, Spanish-looking. He showed me Austrian pigskin handbags, English wool scarves, Swiss watches, Italian silk. Gold jewelry—very chic, very expensive.

I couldn't afford any of it. I was poor now. I bought two small mother-of-pearl frames for my photograph. I was going to give one to my mother and one to Pepi's mother. It would be a sad present, an indication of what the future held.

The salesman walked me through the store, with its pale green walls and thick carpet. The back was far removed from the shopwindow, but I could see natural light. Where from? I looked up and saw a large square of thick glass in the ceiling.

When I was a child, my parents always told me that if I was in trouble or afraid of something, I should immediately look for a policeman. This advice had been drummed into me so deeply that even after the Nazis arrived, if I thought someone was following me in the street, I looked for a policeman, despite knowing that the law didn't protect me anymore.

But someone else was protecting me. Janos, the porter

in our building, was a Party member, and he always told me about things he thought might affect me. He would tell me which districts should be avoided on a certain day, and warned me about certain people of my acquaintance who were in fact Nazi spies. He told me to be inconspicuous, to look poor, to wear no makeup, and to try not to be seen with Walter. Walter was the reason why, that day, he wanted to speak to me in private.

We were in my apartment, where no one could overhear us.

I looked out of the window. There was no romance for me in Vienna's buildings anymore. They were just buildings.

I knew that Janos had something important to tell me, and I knew it couldn't be good. His dark brown eyes avoided mine; plump fingers ran through his thick, dark hair. He shifted his weight from foot to foot. He had short legs. I remembered my father explaining to me that God gave the Austrians short legs because Austria is a mountainous country.

"Janos, come on. Out with it." I smiled. "What's the bad news?"

"They're looking for your chap. They've been here, asking questions. 'Who is she? How long has she lived here? Who lives with her?' I told them you live alone. They wanted to know if you were Jewish. I told them I didn't think so."

Janos looked at me, afraid he had upset me. He had. He saw my fists clench.

"Don't worry, Frau Miller. They believed me, I know they

did. They told me that they had been looking for Walter at Stubenring, but he didn't live there anymore. Someone must have given them your address. Don't worry, please, I'm sure they believed me. They won't come again."

I felt ill, and must have looked it. As Janos left, he invited me downstairs, saying his wife would make me some of her wonderful coffee. But I didn't want to leave the apartment. After he had gone, I went straight into the bathroom, which lay at the back of the building. I opened the window, craned my neck, and peered out. There it was: the glass roof of Hiess's skylight. It covered the whole area of the shaft, about five square meters. I squeezed through the small window and stood outside. A breeze cooled my flushed cheeks, dried my tears. When Walter came home, my plan was in place.

He walked in, beaming, and presented me with a bouquet wrapped in tissue. *Dear God, let him always give me red roses, wherever we may be.*

I told him about Janos's visit, about the men who were looking for him. And then, with an attempt at a lighthearted tone, I told him about my discovery of the glass roof outside the bathroom window. "It's big enough for us to dance on!"

But Walter would not be diverted.

"That's bad news," he said, taking off his glasses and polishing them. "If they're looking for me, I will have to find somewhere else to live. I'm putting you in danger just by being here."

"Rubbish! No one is putting me in danger." I put my fists into my pockets so he couldn't see them. "They don't know that you're here. And if they do come back, you can step out of the bathroom window. They'll never find you there. Who would imagine that anyone could hide outside the window of a first-floor apartment? Here is the safest place for you, believe me. It's a miracle. Another wonderful miracle."

"They'll be able to see me!" Walter shouted hoarsely.

"They won't!" I shouted back. "If you stand very still, close to the wall next to the window, you will be out of sight. But it won't come to that. They won't come back. And even if they do, they won't find you. I promise. You're safe with me."

They did come back—two of them. Janos brought them up. He got Steffi from the workroom. She had instructions to tell them I was asleep.

"Is anybody living with Frau Miller?"

"No one," she replied. "This is a millinery business."

Walter stood outside the window, close to the wall. Not daring to move a muscle. Terrified. He had been stripped of his apartment, his car, his possessions; now he was forced to stand on a roof outside his own home while people hunted for him. I wondered at that moment whether he wished himself dead.

I waited for twenty minutes after the men left, but they didn't return. Still, I hesitated to give Walter the good news; I could picture his face, the humiliation in his eyes. Would I be able to help him? This time, love might not be enough.

I went to the bathroom window and climbed out. There

he was, against the wall, my good, clean, wonderful Walter. Loved, respected, and admired by all. The son of a great inventor. The grandson of the chief rabbi of Prague. My Walter.

I sat down on the glass roof and made him sit down next to me. We didn't say a word. I didn't look at him. I put my head on his hands and held them in my own. Cozy sounds of pigeons. It grew dark. One by one, lights were turned on. The glass roof was lit from inside Hiess. We sat on a sea of light. Dirty clouds swept the sky. Smoke rose from chimney pots. People started cooking their evening meals. I loved Walter more than ever. I dared not imagine what could have happened. To see my Walter taken away, head held high, looking straight ahead. To exist in a world that did not contain Walter seemed pointless.

I wanted him to sit there for as long as he wanted to. No one had the right to call him inside.

6

Divorce laws in Austria were straightforward and reasonable. As long as both parties agreed to terminate the marriage on the grounds of incompatibility, a divorce would be granted. It was a little more difficult with a Jewish marriage. Couples were asked to come three times to the Jewish

Kultusgemeinde—the office in charge of Jewish affairs. There, attempts would be made to persuade them to give the marriage another chance. If, after three visits, the couple still insisted on divorce, permission for the dissolution of the marriage would not be withheld.

I telephoned Pepi and asked him to go there at once and explain that we needed our divorce urgently.

I asked Walter to find out from the British consulate what was happening with his visa. He also wrote to his uncle in London, asking him to go in person to the Home Office.

Pepi was successful; he persuaded them at the *Kultusgemeinde* to make a great exception. We were to call there three times the following week: Monday, Wednesday, and Friday.

On Monday, just before eleven a.m., we arrived there arm in arm. Pepi holds the door open for me. The room is bare. Practical. Not what I was expecting. In front of the window is an impressively large desk. Files and papers are arranged in neat piles. There is a desk chair with arms on one side; two small chairs on the other. A hard, uncomfortable sofa runs along one wall. We have to wait. Pepi holds a chair for me to sit down before sitting himself. I had forgotten how well-brought-up he was.

He goes to fetch coffee and returns with it in two cardboard cups, making a funny face with round, comical eyes. We stop laughing when the desk's occupant arrives. He is tall, thin, with scholarly features, a prominent forehead, and a sardonic smile. He speaks of matrimony, of its happinesses, its shortcomings, about the duty of every married person to keep the "unity of two people," to keep their marriage alive. His voice is cold. Monotonous.

Pepi and I look at each other seriously. The telephone rings. A long conversation takes place. Pepi paces around. Looks through the curtainless windows. I see his broad shoulders, his straight, slim legs.

The man replaces the receiver. He continues his sermon, repeats himself. He is boring us. He mentions our "tender years." Pepi raises his eyebrows, looks at me out of the corner of his eye, lifts his shoulders. He is making me laugh; I have to hold my handkerchief in front of my mouth.

Afterward, he takes me to lunch at Graben. He walks in front of me down the stairs to the *Bierkeller*. Rustic furniture, candlelight. He knows that I like corner tables and leads me to the only one that is unoccupied.

RESERVED, reads the notice. My cool Pepi turns it face-down onto the red and white checked tablecloth. The head-waiter seems to appear from out of the ground, hissing, "Reserved, sir." He takes the money Pepi pushes discreetly into the palm of his hand, pulls out a chair, and holds it there for me to sit down. He does the same for Pepi and leaves, taking the RESERVED notice with him.

I don't know how a man as young as Pepi acquired such worldly manners.

7

I am going to visit my parents. The taxi passes the house where Elsa used to live. She was my very best friend at school.

One day, Elsa and I were in the park. The sun was shining through the trees, onto the flowers and the wing of a large, white butterfly lying on the grass. I picked it up, and Elsa started to run.

"No, Trudi, no! Please! Don't come near me! Don't! Throw it away!" she screamed.

I went closer. She stamped her feet, in black patent sandals, tried to lift the skirt of her pink and white gingham dress over her head. The blond plaits tied with pink ribbon on either side of her head were flying.

A new feeling of power came over me. I terrorized her with it. She was not particularly intelligent. A little fat. I made her run.

Many years later, she took her revenge. Willi was my boyfriend—strong face, good figure, tall, intelligent. At that time, I adored plain-looking men with brains. Mother liked him, too. I had a dream: a cat with a smooth, black coat stared at me, motionless. Green eyes, full of fire and bad intentions. Elsa's eyes. Dreaming of cats means an underhand attack. A lie. Danger.

She and Willi were meeting in secret.

Later on, they married and went to live in Berlin. I heard they died in a concentration camp.

I learned never to trust a woman where men are involved.

Mother's best friend, Alma, a society photographer, once said to me, "Trudi, you are a very discreet girl. You never ask where my husband is. Soon, you will be a young lady and will have lots of men around you. Maybe you will marry one of them. Here is some advice from a good friend with a lot of experience. Never leave your man on his own."

I never did. No other woman ever got hold of Walter.

The taxi stops outside my parents' building. They are waiting for me at their window. I climb up to the third floor, and they are standing in their open doorway.

I haven't been here since Hitler's invasion three months ago. The flat feels different, although everything is the same: the silver-gray bedroom, my room with the large brass bed and white furniture, the blue hall, the long red and blue Persian runner patterned with large green birds that used to frighten me when I was little. My mother points at the piano in the sitting room. "Should I sell it?" she asks.

"No, Mother. Only if you really need money, or are about to leave the country."

"Will we? Leave?" she asks. Her eyes are burning blue question marks.

"I promise, Mother, I'll get you out. Trust me." I put my arm around her and kiss her. She is so thin. "I wouldn't leave you behind."

Did I realize what I was promising?

We sit at the dining table drinking coffee and eating homemade cake. Mother looks worried, but Father doesn't; he's always calm.

They show me a letter. The Austrian tax office has written to my father asking him to pay an astronomical sum in "outstanding income tax." They are threatening to confiscate the contents of the apartment if the bill is not settled within four weeks.

"Trudi, your father has paid all his taxes. He doesn't owe them anything."

"Do you have the receipts?" I ask.

He produces a bundle of papers. "What do you think we should do?" he asks. "I'm afraid to go over there—I could be arrested." His cigarette ash drops onto the carpet.

"Of course you can't go over there. In any case, isn't the apartment in Mother's name? Could you prove that the apartment and its contents belong solely to Mother?"

My mother is not Jewish.

"We have some proof . . ." Mother says doubtfully.

"Don't worry, Mama, please. I'll talk to my lawyer friend. But you might have to be prepared to go to court . . ."

My tiny, tough, clever mother went to court, all by herself. She won her case. Hitler or not, the judge decided that the flat belonged to her alone.

8

Wednesday at the *Kultusgemeinde* was a repeat performance of Monday's session. It didn't take long. The man didn't try so hard. We went home and had sandwiches and coffee with Walter.

"How did it go?" he asks Pepi. "Have you got rid of her yet?"

"It's not that easy," Pepi replies. "It was only the second session."

"Be patient, my friend. Third time lucky." They both laugh.

It's Friday, the final session. I don't want Walter to notice that I'm upset. I'm very possessive where people are concerned; I can't let go. Especially not of Pepi. He's part of my life.

I remember the first time we drove out to the country. Pepi made a wreath of cornflowers and put it on my head. "I make you my queen," he said. "You're beautiful."

We sat on the grass, listening to the birds, lingering in the sunny meadow. A breeze rustled the trees; in the distance, cows mooed.

We arrive at the *Kultusgemeinde* and are shown into a different room this time. The chairs are more comfortable. The desk is less orderly. There is a vase of wild roses and some photographs of children in shorts playing ball. The window is draped with patterned curtains.

A woman comes in and sits down and smiles at us. Then she moves about in her chair, gets up, turns the cushion over, and sits down again. She grins apologetically, showing her white teeth. Her green eyes are laughing. I like her. She uses her pencil to move the blond fringe from her forehead. Pepi gropes for my hand underneath the desk.

"Well?" the lady asks. "Two people, so young, so lovely." She shakes her head, tries to persuade us. It isn't a sermon; it's the warm, intelligent effort of a young, understanding woman.

"Can you reconsider?" She looks from me to Pepi, then back to me. We shake our heads, say no, feel guilty. Pepi tightens his grip on my hand.

He walks me home. We stop at the entrance to my building and face each other, hands clasped. Suddenly, he releases my hands and walks away. His hair blows in the wind as he turns the corner.

PART FIVE

A Voyage

(London, 1936)

1

Looking through Walter's cupboard, I find a flannel suit of mine. My Tyrolean costume! The one I wore on that trip to London back in June 1936. There was a new king on the throne: Edward VIII.

My small suitcase is packed; I have said good-bye to Walter; I am ready to leave. I have booked a passage on a boat from The Hague to England. I am going to London and from there to Paris to do my buying before returning to Vienna. I have chosen the route from Holland because it is the cheapest.

Frightening news has been coming across the border from Germany. Jews were being persecuted. No one seemed to believe it; no one wanted to. But deep down, part of me did believe it. I wanted to be safe. I wanted Walter to be safe. I wanted to live with him in a free country, far away from Hitler. I was going to England partly to see for myself what it was like.

I looked at myself in the mirror. In those days, it was considered chic to wear Tyrolean outfits for sport and travel. Emerald green braid ran down each side of my slim, gray flannel skirt. My gray flannel jacket had a tiny emerald green stand-up collar, wide revers, and cuffs. The buttons down the front were made of horn. My blouse was white lawn. My small-brimmed, black, silky velour hat was trimmed with a wide emerald green ribbon. Black flat-heeled crocodile shoes and a black crocodile clutch bag completed the outfit. I would have felt less proud of my appearance had I known what was in store for me en route . . .

Austria is landlocked, and I had never seen the sea. I imagined it to be blue and smooth. But today, it is rough. The yellow-painted boat in the harbor lurches up and down; I can't read its name, and it makes me feel giddy even to look at it. I climb up the gangway, and sailors help me on. They speak French among themselves. I am shown to the luggage room, where I take off my hat and sit down.

The engines are noisy and grow louder and louder. My head is splitting, and the smell of oil is making me feel sick. Sailors shout in French. I am on a French cargo boat. *Oh God, who booked this trip for me? How did this happen? I can't remember. I feel sick. The boat is moving. I have to hold on to my seat, tightly, with both hands. No, I can't; I have to hold on to my handbag, which has no handles and contains my pass-port, traveler's checks, money, and jewelry. Why did I bring jewelry? I clutch the bag. The boat pitches.*

Through the open door, I see water sloshing around the deck. I have to be sick. I rush outside, bend over the rail, and vomit. More and more. I can't stop. A sailor stands behind me, shouting in French. I'm so ill I can't understand him.

I wouldn't have understood him no matter what language he had been speaking. I don't care what he's saying. I grip my crocodile bag, pressing it against me. My body is pressed against the railings. The sailor continues to shout. He points to a big ridge in front of the rail. I finally understand; if I bend over the rail, the wind will blow my vomit onto the side of the boat, and he will have to clean it.

I can't move. I'm screwed to the deck. He waves his arms, shouts, "Merde," gives up. He fetches a deck chair and forces me down onto it.

My suitcase and my Tyrolean hat are in the luggage room. It is raining. The water floods over me from the sky and from the sea. I am soaking wet and deathly sick. I don't give a damn about anything except my handbag. People fall off their deck chairs. Shoes fly through the air. Even the sailors are being sick. They say it is the worst crossing for fifteen years.

Wet hair sticks to my face, my makeup. The flannel cloth of my suit has absorbed so much water it weighs a ton. It is caked in vomit. One of my hands clings to the rail, the other clutches my bag. If it slips out of my hands into the raging sea, I will jump in after it!

Eventually, we arrive. I don't move. I can't move. Let them come and get me. Now I know why this route is so cheap.

The London train is waiting. A porter finds my luggage and helps me to my compartment. I still feel dreadful. A young woman offers me brandy. I grab the bottle and take a big sip. Maybe it will help. Anything, I'll take anything if it might make me feel better.

"I know how you feel," she says. "I felt bad myself. Everyone was ill on that wretched boat. Not as ill as you, though. Can I fetch you anything?"

I shake my head and close my eyes. I want to die. Eventually I fall asleep, and I must sleep for quite a while, because when I open my eyes and look out of the window there is no sea, just towns and houses and people in cars. I feel better. I'm still clutching my crocodile bag.

The young woman who gave me the brandy brings me a cup of tea. Her black eyes smile at me; her black curly hair reminds me of my favorite doll. She is flirting with the man sitting next to me. Suddenly, I realize how I must look. I get up, walk to the door, trip over my friend's long legs, and apologize.

I look at my reflection—is it really me? I clean the front of my jacket as best I can. The smell is intolerable. I wash my face, brush my hair, and put on fresh makeup.

Returning to my compartment, I find my neighbor sitting close to my new friend. She must be out of her mind. The man has passed his fifties. He has a haggard face and body, thin gray hair with a yellowish tinge. His fingers are stained with nicotine. I close my eyes and fall asleep again.

When I wake up, we have arrived. I glimpse my reflection in the window. Good God! What a way to arrive in London for the first time!

I call a porter. Walking along the platform, I hear someone call: "Hello! Hello, wait for me!" It is my friend from the train. "Where are you going?" she asks. "Have you booked a room?"

"No, I haven't," I reply, as we walk along. "Have you?"

"No." She shakes her head. "Shall we try together?"

I look at her. She is well dressed. She was kind to me. Why not?

"All right," I say. "What's your name?"

"Shirley. Shirley Levin. It's a Jewish name."

"Is it?" I grin.

The taxi takes us from hotel to hotel. Finally, at the Strand Palace, we find a room—a double room, but it's all they have. It is large, with light blue walls, a royal blue fitted carpet and—thank God!—twin beds. There is a small white desk and two comfortable armchairs. I like the four flower pictures in bright red frames above a small blue sofa.

The next morning, I watch Shirley brush her hair and apply makeup in front of a large mirror.

"I was in Vienna to see my mother," she says. "She lives there with her second husband. I am married to an Australian. We live in Sydney. It's lovely there, but I'm bored. I've come to see what England is like. We might move here with the children. How about you?"

"Something similar."

My friend Doris has given me the telephone number of a young Viennese man, a friend of hers. I ask the clerk to put me through. A man's cultured voice answers.

"Is this Mr. Tony Winkler?"

"Yes, that's me. Can I help you?"

"I bring regards and good wishes from Doris Stoerk."

"Ah, Doris. How is she? Are you visiting from Vienna?"

"Yes; I arrived last night."

"Then I am at your disposal."

We arrange to meet for dinner at my hotel. He asks how he will recognize me.

"You can't miss me." I laugh. "Bright red hair."

I like him as he strides into the bar, tall and thin, late twenties. Usually I find tall men either awkward and shy or arrogant and superior. But Tony Winkler seems to be neither. He sees me at once, comes across the room, hands outstretched in greeting.

"May I?" He sits down.

Intelligent, golden-green eyes look through large glasses. He asks about Doris but doesn't seem very interested. He gives me a nice dinner, ordering beautiful wine. We eat raspberries and cream, stir our coffee. Basking in the soothing effect of the wine, we decide to go for a walk to the river. Moon and stars shine and sparkle. The illuminated Houses of Parliament are reflected in the Thames. Little boats are outlined by small white lights. I miss Walter.

Back at the hotel, I book a call to Vienna. No reply. The telephone rings and rings. Maybe he's asleep. "No reply," says the operator.

If I hadn't telephoned, I wouldn't have known. Now I will not sleep. Why is he not at home? Where is he? With whom? Why?

Love has so many twists and turns. Jealousy is one of them. I'm insanely jealous.

It is midnight. One o'clock. Shirley tiptoes into the room, holding her shoes.

"I'm awake," I say. "You don't have to be quiet."

"Why aren't you asleep?"

I tell her.

"You shouldn't have telephoned," she says.

"I know that now." I look at her. "Where have you been? You can tell me that it's none of my business. It isn't. But having shared a room for a night, one cares a little."

She smells of alcohol. Her lipstick is smudged.

"Look at yourself. You stupid girl. You have a husband, two children, a lovely home. What are you doing?"

"I've done nothing," she sulks.

"You went out with a stranger. Ate and drank with a stranger. In a strange country. And I know who you have been with. He could almost be your grandfather."

"He asked after you," she whispered. "Sends his regards."

She goes to bed. I fall asleep. Next morning, I leave while her head is still buried in the pillows. I have booked a guided tour of the city.

London is beautiful. Majestic. It has class, tradition, elegance. People are charming, polite, and kind. They look prosperous. I think of my poor unemployed Vienna. I think of Walter. I buy him a silk tie.

There are fresh tea roses in my room when I return. No card. Tony Winkler telephones at six thirty. He invites me to dinner. Against my better judgment, I accept. Maybe I am more like Shirley than I think. Where was Walter last night?

The embrace takes place at the side entrance to the hotel. It is dark. He takes me by surprise. I feel no attraction, no curiosity. I want to get away from him. He makes me feel dirty as his arms tighten around me, his face moves nearer to mine. His blond hair touches mine. My arms stretch out to push him away. He pulls me closer, presses his thigh against mine. He is aroused. It is revolting. Gently, with my palms, I push his face away, twist out of his grip, and run inside.

Next morning, Shirley is still asleep when I am ready to leave. I want to say good-bye, exchange addresses.

"I'll miss you!" she says. She is truly upset.

"Be a good girl, and be sensible," I say.

"I am," she says with pride. "You were quite right. I found myself a much younger man!"

I set off to Paris in my express-cleaned suit. I longed for my home, my routine, my friends, my workroom. I longed for Walter. I rushed through my work in Paris and cut my stay short.

As my train pulled slowly into the station in Vienna, I saw Walter on the platform. My heart walked in front of me to greet him. On the way to my apartment, I told him all about London.

"Walter, the money lies in the street, waiting to be picked

up. The place, the people—I love it all. We could be happy there!"

Walter just smiled. "Why don't you go first? Get everything ready, and I will follow?" He spoke as if I were a child, his tone benevolent. I was hurt, and never raised the subject again.

I never asked him where he had been that night.

PART SIX

"Walter, We Must Run"

(Vienna, 1938)

1

The workroom door is half-open. "Hello," says Walter, putting his head inside.

"*Guten Morgen*, Herr Ehrlich," say my girls. They like him.

"Want some lunch?" I put my arm through his. We go to the kitchen.

"Any news?" Walter asks, dipping some radishes into salt and helping himself to some thinly sliced black bread. I have prepared it as he likes it, well-buttered and topped with finely chopped chives.

"Your sister telephoned. They're all right."

"Good."

"She wants us to go over there. She says we're neglecting them."

"Why doesn't she come here?"

"You wouldn't want that! It's much too dangerous here. She would have to bring the boy. He's only three. And she's right—we haven't seen them for ages."

We eat hot frankfurters with French mustard and freshly

grated horseradish. Coffee. Walter lights a cigarette, strokes my hand. He looks like the cat who got the cream.

"Guess what?" he purrs. He is interrupted by the wretched cuckoo clock. The cuckoo looks really vicious to me now. Maybe he's a Nazi?

"Guess," he insists.

"If it's something good, just tell me," I say.

"It's something very, very important to me. Something I wouldn't like to live without. *Couldn't.*"

"Walter. Please."

"We're getting married. I've booked the date."

"So what?" I say and burst into tears.

2

The delicatessen at the corner is the largest in Vienna. The only one that sells pineapples from South Africa, Indian tea, English bacon, Scottish smoked salmon. Everything looks wonderful. I want to buy French raspberry jam. A salesman in a white linen jacket stands by a machine and cuts Polish Krakauer into paper-thin slices. Polish Krakauer is my favorite—ham sausage, hung up to dry until it is very hard. On a shelf along the wall are jars containing every spice in the world. A huge aluminum bucket holds peeled Portuguese almonds. A man buys a large bottle of Hungarian apricot brandy.

We haven't had it for a long time. My eyes move to the shelves, looking for a smaller bottle. Then it hits me: I can't afford even that. A light is cleverly directed at cold meats inside the glass counter. It makes the meat look irresistibly pink and fresh. There is the smell of freshly baked bread.

The place is packed; I have to wait to be served. A girl, brown hair, white apron, makes dainty parcels, hands them to a lady, and says, "*Danke schön, gnädige Frau.*"

I stand at the counter, looking at the contented faces around me. They haven't had to get used to hiding, to being afraid. The ground beneath their feet is solid.

I hear the loud voice of a young woman. Too loud, considering her Jewish accent. She has red hair. When she laughs, her full lips open, showing small, white teeth. Her eyes are china blue. She puts her arm around the shoulders of the man next to her. Pepi's shoulder. I draw back into the farthest corner of the shop. They can't see me. I hear my heart beat. I feel as though it is choking me. *Why? He's free. He isn't your husband anymore.* But he's still my Pepi! *You have another man now. A man you really love, a man you are to marry in a few days' time. You're jealous!* No, I'm not! *Do you love him?* Yes, like a brother! *Then let him go.* He's mine!

She links arms with Pepi and presses her head into his shoulder. He's nervous. She flirts. She's fighting for him.

I want to shoot her. Suddenly she frees her arm to point a bright red nail at the Edam cheese; she wants to touch it. Pepi stops her. He is embarrassed.

The saleslady puts their purchases into a paper bag. She doesn't make dainty parcels for them. She hands the bag to Pepi and ignores the girl.

Pepi, she isn't good enough for you.

3

I'm alone. We have arranged to spend the night apart. We meet tomorrow morning at ten o'clock at the register office. The ceremony is at eleven.

It is midnight, and I'm still awake. Tomorrow I will marry Walter. Tomorrow, 13 July 1938. What a date for a wedding. But the number 13 doesn't worry me. Any day I marry Walter will be a lucky day. It will be a simple civil ceremony. Not like when Pepi and I got married. That wedding was arranged by his parents. I remember my mother in silver-gray chiffon, large diamond earrings. She looked beautiful. Father, tall and elegant. He had made my wedding present himself: a necklet of South American topazes, set in circles of tiny diamonds. "To match your goldfish hair," he said.

On his arm, I entered the synagogue, a garden of white

and yellow flowers. Father admired my pale lilac tulle dress, the small, veiled hat made of violets. Father had taste and style.

It all seemed like a dream. An organ played soft music, far away. *Is this my wedding?* There were hundreds of people. I couldn't see their faces. Mother Miller, under the chuppah, wore black with white roses and pearls. She gave me a sweet smile. Father Miller looked miserable. His black hat, too large, slipped over his ears. Pepi tried to catch my eye. He stood next to the rabbi.

The clock in the sitting room chimes. It is two in the morning. I still can't sleep. What will I look like tomorrow? Perhaps I won't wear my white dress. I'll wear navy blue. I'm not in the mood to dress up, but I want to look nice. I hope, in years to come, Walter will remember. *Years to come.* Who can think so far ahead, when even a year from now seems an age away. Everything was so different when I married Pepi. People bought a home, brought up their children, and celebrated their silver wedding in the same house. Everything was forever. Most people I know now don't know where they will be in a few months' time—a few days' time. They don't know if they will make it through tomorrow.

My parents believed in God but were not very religious. I didn't know much about Jewish weddings. I listened to Hebrew words I didn't understand. I tried to listen to the rabbi. He looked important in his black hat, white and black striped shawl.

A glass, wrapped in white cloth, was placed on the floor.

Pepi smashed it under his foot. This is the Jewish symbol of a husband's commitment to protect his wife. *Pepi will protect me. Pepi will protect me.* I wasn't thinking clearly anymore.

Pepi held out the ring. He put it on my finger. We kissed. Dutifully, I kissed everybody. It was over. People were congratulating me.

Why did I cry?

Daylight creeps around the blue velvet curtains, lacing their edges.

I stand in front of my mirror. I wear my navy blue crepe de chine dress. It has a small décolleté and short sleeves. The skirt is draped across to the left hip, held in place by a huge white rose.

Doris comes in with a white flower toque, holding it with great care. It is made entirely of large rose petals. Steffi suggests that I put all my hair inside the hat. A fine green veiling covers my eyes.

"How chic it looks, madame," Steffi says. She hands me my long, white kid gloves.

"No jewelry?" Doris asks.

"No," I reply.

The girls are more excited than I am.

4

Walter and I stand in front of the register office. Not a memorable building. We have no witnesses. We don't want anyone to know. These days, no one tells anyone anything.

The ceremony has little to do with a wedding. It is soulless, mass-produced, commercialized, like the room we sit in, which is like a dentist's waiting room. We are a little afraid. Behind the huge desk sits a morose, unfriendly man. The floor is covered in linoleum. There are no curtains at the window. There are notices tacked to the walls. Walter takes my hand, puts it in his pocket, and holds it there.

There are several couples waiting in front of us. Suddenly, I am excited. I squeeze Walter's hand as we move toward the desk.

The cold voice asks, "Will you take this man to be your wedded husband?"

"I will," I whisper.

We are outside, crossing the road. Walter stops in the middle of the traffic.

"Do me a favor, darling. Take your hat off."

I do. My hair tumbles across my face and over my shoulders.

"Much better." He laughs as we run to the other side.

5

Nobody tells anyone anything. People vanish without saying good-bye. Everyone is afraid. We try to be as inconspicuous as possible. Drawing attention to oneself is dangerous.

But I can't possibly leave without seeing Pepi's family. His parents. They are like my second parents, and it might be the last chance I have.

We drive to Döbling, on the outskirts of Vienna. I remember going there with Pepi for the first time. I was impressed and apprehensive when we drew up outside his parents' palatial house. We turned into the drive. Wide steps led up to huge double doors. I wanted to go home. Pepi laughed, took my hand, and led me inside.

In the hall was a magnificent Dutch commode in dark, shiny wood. It held a white, smiling china Buddha. Hedi, Pepi's younger sister, raced across the hall to be the first to greet me. Her amber eyes.

Friedl, his elder sister, stood in the doorway watching me. The sun shone through tall French windows and lit up her red hair, the most vibrant red I had ever seen. She walked gracefully. She took my face in her hands and made me look into her leaf green eyes. Her pink mouth touched my cheeks. She smiled and took my hand. "Come, Trudi. Meet Father." She became my favorite sister-in-law. We were like sisters.

* * *

Now I feel sorry for the Millers' house. It has lost its shine; it is crying. It has seen so much happiness, that house to which we all returned again and again. One by one, its occupants are leaving. Soon the house will be all alone.

Pepi's mother rushes out of the kitchen. There are no servants left, yet still she has a bunch of keys hanging from a bunch around her waist.

"Welcome home, my child," she says, stroking my hair.

Pepi's father, as always, sits on the green sofa that stands on the large, red Bokhara carpet. He is nearly eighty now. He looks at me over the top of his glasses and says, "Goodbye, my child. Have a lovely time." He thinks I am going on holiday.

My heart is heavy. Pepi's mother walks me to the front door, puts her arms around me, and holds me for a long time. Pepi drives me home. He has decided to stay with his parents until they are able to leave.

The members of the Miller family who were already in New York City eventually managed to arrange a passage to Havana for their parents. The plan was that they could wait there in safety until their quota numbers came up and they could enter the United States. But Pepi's father died before they could leave Vienna. His mother, seventy years old, went to Havana all by herself. For eight months she lived there on her own, without friends, not understanding a word of the language, until she was finally allowed to join her children.

6

As I enter my building, Janos steps out of the shadows. He has been waiting for me. He looks around furtively.

"I have seen him again," he whispers, "the man who was asking about your new husband. He didn't see me—he didn't come into the building. I just saw him in the street." He looks at me with his innocent brown eyes.

Oh, Janos. Dear Janos. Say something good.

I can't speak. I touch his cheek, put my finger to my lips, and go upstairs. Walter is out. I stand at the window of my sitting room, looking down at Kohlmarkt.

Where is he? Why isn't he home yet? He has gone out to collect some kind of plastic prototype that he needs for a design. He told me, "This prototype will be the basis for my next business."

I take refuge in my workroom. The girls are busy: steaming, ironing, sewing, singing. They exchange looks when they see me. Dolly borrows the model hat that Maria is copying. It is for a customer named Frau Schumacher; Dolly imitates her, tilting the hat at an angle so that it almost covers her right eye. She puts a pencil in her mouth, pretending it is a cigarette, puffing imaginary smoke. I join in the laughter.

I try on some straw hats. The fittings are good. The room radiates industry and good humor. But it doesn't help the sinking feeling inside me. *Walter, come home. Please.*

I warn Steffi and Doris. They know what to do if the men come calling again. I go into the showroom. The lovebirds are courting noisily. Feathers proudly puffed out, they turn their heads from side to side, cheeping. I poke my finger through the bars of their cage, and they peck at my nail. Steffi comes in: "Madame, the lady from upstairs is here. She wants to talk to you."

"Thank you, Steffi. Show her into the sitting room."

Anna, my neighbor, is Russian, about fifty. She is thin, tiny. She was a prima ballerina once; she fell in love, gave up her career, and now is a widow, lonely and sad. She is fond of me and adores Walter.

"Frau Trudi, I noticed a man hanging around yesterday—short, stocky, gray hair. He was standing on the other side of the road and seemed to be watching the entrance to our building; he was there for more than an hour. Then this morning, he stopped me in the street. 'Excuse me,' he said, 'I am looking for Herr Ehrlich. I believe he lives in this building. Can you tell me where to find him?' I told him I know no one of that name. 'He's very good-looking,' the man said. 'Dark hair, blue eyes. We believe he might be connected with a Frau Miller who lives on the first floor.' 'I know Frau Miller well,' I said, 'but I've never heard of this person. I'm sorry, I can't help you.' He left me alone after that. I'm really sorry. It's bad news, I know. I hope it will be all right in the end. You can trust me. I'm your friend."

I realize that Walter mustn't come back to No. 11. I need to warn him. I wonder if he might be at the Café Rebhuhn—

he always said it was a good place to meet his friends because he thought it was unlikely that they would make a big arrest in front of so many people "They try to fool people that everything is normal," he said. "They try to do everything in secret."

I telephone my parents. "Mother, don't ask questions, please—Walter needs to stay with you tonight."

"Why, darling? What's happened?"

"Please don't ask questions, Mother. Walter will explain. I'm sorry I can't come—I might be followed." She is shocked. I am very upset. I say good-bye.

I am terrified the man will come back when Walter is at home. The glass roof might not work again. This time they will search every corner, every cupboard, every place where he might hide. Every cupboard? Good God! Walter's clothes! I need to move them. Where? In a panic, I telephone Pepi.

"Pepi, you need to come over, quickly. I'm in trouble. Help me. Walter's suits—his books—it's too much . . ."

"Calm down, darling," he says. "Calm down and tell me what's going on."

"I can't talk now. Please come. Come at once. Please."

I run into the bedroom, take down Walter's suitcases and start to pack his clothes. The shirt with the blue stripes, his favorite. On the hanger is the white one he wore yesterday. The blue suit needs cleaning. All his shoes need cleaning. I pack them. I pack the beautiful red cardigan I gave him for his birthday. His razor, his shaving brush. His files of business correspondence. There must be no trace of him in the apartment, nothing that connects him with this place in any way. Oh, God, his glasses!

What if they are waiting for Walter downstairs? If they catch him coming into the building, it's the end. Walter will simply vanish. My legs give way, and I sink onto the bed.

The doorbell rings. I run into Pepi's arms and howl into his shoulder. He strokes my hair, whispers to me, trying to calm me down. I don't hear what he is saying, but after a while I stop crying. I show him the suitcases I have packed and tell him what has happened.

"Please take them away, Pepi. Now. If anyone stops you, the cases belong to you, they are yours. They have been here since before we divorced. Understand?"

"Don't worry, darling. Everything will be all right."

"Please, Pepi, hurry!"

Walter comes home. He wasn't seen.

"Walter, thank God you're back, but you have to leave. I don't know how, but you have to. You're in terrible danger."

"What's happened? You're shaking. What's the matter?"

"The man, he was here again, asking for you . . ."

"How do you know?"

"Anna told me. He asked her if she knew you."

Walter tries to hide his fear.

We have to get out of here, out of Vienna, or he will break. He has been singled out. Why? He hasn't done anything wrong. Everyone loves him. He has no enemies.

We are sitting on the floor, side by side, holding hands. I remember walking with him across frozen snow. The crunch. The sky was blue, and the air was cold, bubbly as champagne. The sun was shining on Vienna. The snow glittered.

7

"Hello, Father. How's everybody?"

"Fine. Do you want to speak to—"

"No! I can't speak to anybody."

"Darling, everything's fine. Don't worry."

"OK, Papa. Give my love to—"

It is dark. I draw the curtains. It's the first night since we were married that I am in bed without Walter. He's safe with my parents—or as safe as anyone can be at the moment. I have locked the door, locked all the windows. If the doorbell rings, I won't answer.

The telephone rings. It isn't the signal I have arranged with my parents, Walter, and Pepi. I'm frightened. They could come anytime, demand that I open up.

I try to read a magazine, but I can't concentrate. I turn off the light and put my head under the pillow, but I can't sleep.

The persecution of Walter is coming from someone specific, someone with a grudge. If the Nazis wanted to arrest him, they would have had him long ago. The person who wants Walter must know a Nazi, someone high up in the Party, and is prepared to pay. Who is it? Who wants revenge, and for what?

Is it a woman? A woman scorned?

It is quiet in my bedroom. No traffic or voices filter through to the back of the building. I dream my childhood dream. I'm picking wild strawberries in the woods. The largest and ripest are hidden under small shrubs and tree stumps. I collect them in my jam jar. I don't eat a single one; they are for Mother. Usually I'm happy when I wake up from this dream, but not this time. There's a weight on my chest, and I can't breathe.

It's raining. The wind hurls slabs of water against the windowpanes. I pull the blanket over my head.

I dream that I am cut out of a large sheet of thick cardboard. I am an outline. Mother carries me under her arm; I stick out front and back. She takes me home. I wake up in a cold sweat. *Mother. I want to go home.*

I pile up pillows under my head. I turn over and over and over. It comes to me in a flash; suddenly, I feel certain that I know who our persecutor is. Herr Hans Holler. Monocle, barrel chest, short legs. A name-dropper, a social climber. Herr Holler was a member of the sports club Pepi and I used to go to when we were married. We would play tennis there, and bridge, and go to the socials. Herr Hans Holler was keen on me. He would follow me around the place, sitting close to me and staring. Sometimes I would find him behind me, sniffing at my neck, my hair. Because of him, I stopped going to the club.

Then came Hitler, and Herr Hans Holler reappeared. I would see him at Demel. He came over to my table, sat next to me. I couldn't get up and move elsewhere. Herr Hans Holler was now a Nazi.

He telephoned and asked me to dinner. When I declined, he became aggressive. He didn't ask me again; he ordered me to accompany him. I had several dinners with him. We would always meet at the restaurant. I knew that he couldn't hold his drink, so I would make him drunk. Then I would take a taxi, drop him in front of his house, and go home.

One day, Herr Holler said, "Tomorrow, we will have dinner in my flat." His watery blue eyes were blades; his thin, blond hair was damp.

"I can't do that, Herr Holler. I am a lady," I said.

"I won't do anything you don't want me to do. I want you to walk across my bedroom, naked, with your silver fox fur around your neck."

"I can't do that."

"My dear, you have a father, a husband, and a boyfriend. Whom do you love the most? You are intelligent enough to know what I am saying. Think it over. I will telephone you tomorrow."

Herr Hans Holler never telephoned me again. It seemed a miracle, until someone told me that he had been accused of mixing with Jews and was banished to the provinces.

Now I am certain that he is back, and that he is the cause

of our present trouble. We have to get out of Vienna, out of Austria. But we can do nothing without the American or English visas.

We have to wait.

We can't afford to wait.

8

I take a taxi to the Czechoslovakian embassy. Paying the driver, I'm shocked. On the pavement is a crowd of hundreds of people. A woman standing next to me says, "There are SS men at the entrance. They are letting people in two at a time."

I learned at that moment that you must never allow yourself to be one of a crowd. You have to do something on your own.

"Fräulein." I turn around. My taxi driver is behind me. "Fräulein, what is it you want here?"

"I need a visa for my husband," I say, my eyes filling with tears.

"Come on, fräulein." He smiles. "Don't cry. I can help you."

"How?"

"Come on." He opens the taxi door for me. "Jump in. I think your troubles are over."

He takes me back to Kohlmarkt. In the building next to the Vaterländische Front is a small travel agency.

"Go up there," my driver says, pointing to the first floor. "He can help you. He specializes in taking groups to Pistian in Czechoslovakia. It's a spa, mud baths—good for people with rheumatism. It's easy to put in an extra passport."

I get out and pay him.

"Thank you," I say. "I will never forget you."

We shake hands. "Good luck, fräulein," he says. "You're too young to die."

Upstairs, I come face-to-face with a tall, blond, young German.

"Can I help you?" He has a charming smile. "Won't you sit down?" He holds out a chair for me. "What can I do for you?"

I explain the situation.

"Is your husband a Jew?"

"What a question!" I laugh.

"I'm afraid I can't help you. They don't give visas to Jews."

"No one will know he's Jewish! Just put his passport with all the others. Nobody will notice. If anyone asks, you can say that you know him, that he has to go on a business trip, that he's in a hurry and can't find his birth certificate, but you know he's all right. Will you do that? Please?"

He hesitates, and my heart nearly stops.

"I might be able to help you," he says, "but the official at the Czech passport office will want a lot of money."

"How much is a lot?" I ask. He mentions a huge sum. "I

haven't got that sort of money," I say. "You know that our bank accounts have been frozen. All my customers left, owing me money. I might be able to ask friends for help—I might be able to manage it—but I certainly won't be able to find more than that. Can we do this deal now, immediately?"

"Today is Tuesday," he says. "I am going to the Czech embassy on Thursday morning. Where will you be at one o'clock?"

I give him the number of Café Rebhuhn. "I'll be waiting for your call," I say. "Good-bye. Thank you."

I haven't the money to pay him. I am going to have to sell the large diamond clip that Pepi gave me. I know he won't mind. I telephone my parents and ask them to come over to No. 11 straightaway. "Take a taxi, please," I say to Mother. "I need to speak to Father urgently."

When they arrive, I explain. "How much can I get for it?" I ask, handing Father the clip.

He walks to the window and examines it with his loupe. I have seen him do this so many times. His kind face is serious, his dark brown eyes intense. Thick, white hair. *Father, Mother, how can I bear to leave you behind?* My tiny mother, once so strong, now so helpless. And I will be leaving them alone in this dangerous place.

If Father is right—and he always is—I will have enough money to buy our freedom. Our lives. And—with the help of God—the lives of my parents.

"Don't go by yourself, Truderl," my father says. "They cheat Jewish people."

I don't look Jewish. Still, they might guess. He advises me to let the Retzabecks, my parents' closest friends, sell the clip for me. They are Catholics and can be trusted.

I am taking a risk. If the man at the travel agency doesn't get the visa, I will have sold the clip at a low price and lost money for nothing. But I have no choice.

But everything goes well. The clip is sold. The money comes to more than I need. I arrange to meet Walter at midday on Thursday at the Café Rebhuhn.

I have a lot to do. If the travel agent gets the visa for Walter, I will be able to leave with him; I will say I am going on my sales trip to London. I will be able to take only one suitcase and one piece of hand luggage. I have to be careful that nobody suspects I am not coming back. Only Steffi will know the truth.

I wander through the apartment. What shall I take? I love everything in my apartment. How much of it can I fit into a single suitcase?

Is this what we have come to? Here I am, in the middle of my sitting room, holding my favorite oval snuffbox. On the outer lid, enameled in beautiful colors, Cupid guards two half-naked lovers in a sunny meadow. A brown and white dog observes the scene. On the inside lid, a soldier woos a fair-haired girl who leans against a tree. He holds her hand tenderly. They will have to stay in their idyll. There's my pale blue Persian pottery. My Louis XV onyx clock, a family heirloom. It chimes softly every half hour. My paintings—they are not valuable; they are colorful, decorative.

Some of the best things that would not be missed by visitors we have put in storage already: Walter's two carpets from Stubenring, some furniture, silver, bed and table linen. A large Brussels lace tablecloth with twelve napkins like transparent clouds woven by spiders. I decide to have these belongings, along with the clock, sent on to Holland to be kept in storage there. The storage agreement is in Walter's name.

It is Thursday. Midday. They are all here in the café. Good-natured Beppo, loyal Tony, and Poldi, my enemy. A blond man I don't know, and my Walter. They sit at their usual table, the large one in the corner. Café Rebhuhn looks the same as ever—relaxed, old-fashioned, a place for intellectuals to meet and talk. Round tables with dark gray marble tops, wrought-iron legs. Banquettes covered with dark red plush. Cigarette burns: the sign of life in a place. Plain, brown, uncomfortable bentwood chairs. Nothing has changed here since the reign of Franz Josef.

I haven't seen Walter for four days. He sees me first, stands up, grins. His eyes sparkle through the thick haze of smoke. He hurries toward me, knocks over a chair, embraces me. His friends greet me warmly: "Hello, Trudi, how are you?" "Congratulations Frau Ehrlich!" "Where would you like to sit?" We kiss, shake hands, laugh. Walter puffs out his chest with pride, like my lovebirds. For the first time, I realize properly that I am now Frau Ehrlich.

They order Turkish coffee for me, a speciality of the house:

finely ground coffee and demerara sugar boiled together, with two drops of cold water added at the end to settle the grounds. They give me the best seat. Walter sits next to me, holds my hand. My soldier from the snuffbox.

Suddenly Walter says, "It's one o'clock."

Everyone falls silent. They know why I am here. We wait.

"Frau Ehrlich, telephone." The waiter moves the table to let me out. I feel faint.

"Hello?"

"Frau Ehrlich?" It is the German.

"Yes." I try to keep my voice steady. The floor of the kiosk is littered with cigarette butts. I see the torn pages of the open telephone directory.

"I am at the Czech embassy," the German says. "The official wants more money. What shall I do?"

"I told you when I was in your office that I would have to borrow some of the money. And now he wants more? I haven't got it. I'm terribly sorry. You know how important the visa is to me—it's a matter of life and death. Really. Believe me. Please."

A pause. "Very well," the German says. "I will try again, but don't blame me if I can't get it. I will meet you at my office in half an hour."

Now he has frightened me. Maybe he was telling the truth. I am gambling with our lives.

"He telephoned from the embassy?" Walter asks. "How can he be back in his office in half an hour? It takes at least forty-five minutes, door-to-door."

My heart is pounding as I climb the stairs to the first floor of the building on Kohlmarkt. The German hands me Walter's passport with the visa inside. He smiles impishly. *Oh*, I think, *You bastard, you had it all along.* I cross the road to No. 11, looking around me carefully, still afraid of the man who was looking for Walter. I go to the kitchen, make myself a cup of coffee, and sit on the window seat. The cuckoo calls three o'clock. *I won't miss you*, I think. *Your hard, shrill voice. Your beady, soulless eyes.* The sun shines through the windows. The clouds are dispersing. We are free to go.

I telephone Walter at the Café Rebhuhn. "Everything is all right, darling," I say. "Stay where you are. Pepi will come for you. I love you."

I am calm. Pepi and I will smuggle Walter out of the Café Rebhuhn and into the car. I still have some packing to do. And I have to say good-bye to the girls, without giving away the fact that I might never see them again. They helped to pack a collection of 150 model hats that were sent to England for my business trip.

"Have a good time," Dolly says. "Bring back lots of orders."

"Good luck, take it easy." Doris smiles. "Auf Wiedersehen!"

"Auf Wiedersehen," I say.

I ask Steffi to come into the kitchen. I take off my gold locket that I wear on a long, black velvet ribbon and put it around her neck. We cry. Steffi tells me she will look after my parents and do all she can to help them. She will keep the business going for as long as possible, despite the risk of retribution from the Gestapo when they finally realize that I am not coming back. And she promises to keep in touch with Pepi.

"Steffi, before you close down, take anything you want from here—the workroom, the showroom, and the flat. I want you to have it all. Steffi, dear Steffi, I'll never forget you." Tears run down our cheeks.

The Prague train leaves at five thirty p.m. It is now four o'clock. Pepi will be here any moment. I'm dressed, ready to go, and I'm relieved when he arrives. He carries my suitcase and my hand luggage downstairs. I watch from the window as he puts them in the boot of his car, next to Walter's case. I look for a short, stocky man with gray hair.

"Please, God, don't let it go wrong," I pray out loud.

Pepi runs back upstairs, pulls me away from Steffi, and rushes me into the car. I look through the back window and say good-bye to No. 11.

We drive to the back entrance of Café Rebhuhn. Pepi strolls through the corridors to the front, signals to Walter, walks him to the back door, and pushes him quickly into the car. Walter doesn't look at me as Pepi drives off.

The station is busy. The porter puts the luggage into our compartment.

We stand on the platform. Walter's face is white and strained. He hasn't said a word since he left the café.

Pepi embraces him. "If you don't make her happy," he says, "I'll break your neck."

He embraces me quickly and hurries away. I have to put my hand over my mouth to stop myself from sobbing.

9

We are on the train. My thoughts are tumbling about, from childhood to marriage, from divorce to remarriage, to goodbyes, to my parents. I have left them all alone. I used to find them tiresome. Now I want to look after them forever.

When I was a child, I had the best of everything—holidays, clothes, teachers, nannies, maids, doctors. But I wanted my parents to kiss me, to stroke my hair, to put their arms around me. I wanted to feel important. They didn't understand.

I think of my mother's thin neck, the lines under her eyes. I saw her clean her spectacles with the hem of her skirt. I saw large veins on my father's elegant hands.

I look out of the window at the busy platform. A girl in a Tyrolean outfit kisses her parents. I want to take Walter's hand, get out of the train, walk along the platform, through the turnstile, into the street, catch a bus to Kärntner Ring, walk down Kärntnerstrasse, look in the windows of Gardos, the Hungarian who makes my shoes. Walk across Graben, past Knize, Walter's tailor, turn into Kohlmarkt, greet every shop, every street corner. Past the jeweler, into No. 11. I still have my keys. I walk through my lovely apartment, my workroom, say hello to my lovebirds . . .

I am on the train, leaving.

I am the lucky one, so they say.

PART SEVEN

A New Life

(London, 1938)

1

The train crawls. We have yet to face German passport control. Our Austrian passports are still valid. On mine, I'm still
Frau Gertrud Miller. I'm on a business trip, selling model
hats in order to bring English pounds to Nazi Germany. I
sit opposite Walter Ehrlich, a stranger in a salt-and-pepper
suit. Next to him, two elderly ladies dressed in black whisper
together. On my right sits a tall man with a squashed nose
like a boxer's. A thin man sits next to him.

We have gone through the outskirts of Vienna. I take a last
look at the trees and the cornfields. Walter's eyes are closed.

"We'll be at the border soon," says the man next to him.

Walter opens his eyes. We exchange looks.

It is forbidden to take more than ten Austrian schillings in
cash out of the country. I have letters of credit for my business
expenses. The English, French, and Czechoslovakian visas are
in my passport. I wear tiny diamond studs in my earlobes, my
Omega gold watch, and an antique gold bracelet. The topaz
necklace that Father made for me is in my handbag.

*Please God, don't let them take it away. Help us to cross the
border safely.*

The train slows down, screeches, rattles, and stops. The conductor races through our compartment. The thin man yawns, clasps his fingers behind his head, stares out of the misty window. It is raining. Walter looks at his watch, doors open and close, people walk along the platform. A man in a navy blue suit enters our compartment, looks at us, and closes the door.

"*Passkontrolle!*" the German says.

He holds out his hand to Walter. "*Pass?*" Walter gives it to him. He scrutinizes each page and hands it back to him. He repeats this procedure with everyone in the compartment, leaving me to the last. I feel faint. He takes my passport, looks at each page, looks at me, checks each page again. Our lives depend on the whim of a single Nazi.

"Which is your luggage?" he asks.

I point it out to him.

"Is this all you have?"

I nod.

He's still not satisfied. He stares at my face. Is he trying to decipher whether or not I am Jewish? He returns my passport, opens the door slowly, hesitates, glances back, then leaves. A few moments later, we see him on the platform, walking away. Walter smiles at me.

Shortly after we left Austria, a new German law came into force: Jews had to have a large red *J* stamped in their passports.

The train moves slowly across the border. It is over.

2

We arrive in Prague, put our cases in left luggage, and rush to the nearest café. Walter finds the number of his uncle Moritz in the telephone directory. Ten minutes later, under an umbrella, through sheets of heavy July rain, he arrives at the café. He is pudgy, homely looking. His shoes and turnups are soaked.

"Children, how wonderful to see you! Ilsa is telephoning everyone. We're so thankful you are here. Don't worry about a thing; we'll look after you. Why didn't you tell us that you were coming? We're so happy. Two lovely young people. Two of our family! What a miracle! How did you do it? No—it doesn't really matter; you're here, that's all that counts."

Ilsa welcomes us with tears in her eyes. Leon looks like his dark-eyed father. Rosi, a tiny, red-haired doll, wears a short, pink and white gingham dress trimmed with white rickrack. She looks at me with big eyes—she has been told that we have escaped from Hitler, the Monster.

While we are in Prague, we are invited every night to a different family member's home. They push money into Walter's pockets and take us shopping for new clothes.

"Stay in Prague with us," Aunt Dinah begs. "We'll open a business for you, Truderl. We can find you lovely premises."

"We'll give you all the money you need to get started," Uncle Karli says. "Prague could do with a decent milliner!"

I explain that I can't possibly live in a country that has a frontier with Germany. They don't understand. They feel as safe as we did before the flood of German Jewish refugees arrived in Vienna. They rented a flat for us, tried to persuade us to stay.

Walter suggested to them that they should send the children to schools in England. I offered to look after them.

"Then, if anything should happen, they'll be safe," Walter pleaded. "Between England and Germany is the sea. If Hitler doesn't invade Czechoslovakia, I'll bring them back."

We try to warn them.

The documentation for my business trip to London expires at the end of September; it is now the 24th. We are waiting for Walter's British visa and are growing anxious. Finally, it arrives, but because people are panicking about a possible German occupation of the Sudetenland, no seats are available on any of the airplanes leaving Prague. It is impossible to go by train, as the route passes through Germany. People are so desperate to leave that they adopt extreme strategies. A distant cousin of mine tells me that she and twenty of her friends have bought an airplane to get them out of Prague. She apologizes that there is no room for us; I don't tell her that we couldn't have afforded it anyway.

Walking across Wenzelsplatz, I see an Air France sign. "Let's try here," I suggest.

Walter shakes his head. "It's no use."

"We have to try! Doing nothing will get us nowhere!"

The young fellow at the desk looks good-natured. I explain the situation and show him my documents.

"You can see, they expire at the end of this month. If I'm caught here, even for a few days, they will be void. You know what that means."

"I wish I could help, but there are no seats available on any plane, at any time. People are leaving Prague as if fleeing the plague. If the Germans come, I'll be caught here myself—I have no way out."

A thought struck me—I don't know how. It could have come only from God.

"Where is the next plane into Prague coming from?"

"Vienna."

I am certain that no one will fly into a country that is about to be overrun by Germany. There will have been cancellations. Seats from Vienna should be available.

"Please," I beg. "Telephone Vienna and try to book two seats from there. I'll pay for the call."

Walter picks up my gloves from the floor where I have dropped them and makes me sit down. He holds my hand.

The young man walks into the back office. Through the glass door, I see him pick up the telephone. He shakes his head and seems to be arguing with someone. I clench my fists.

"Calm down, darling," Walter whispers. My gaze is fixed

on the glass door. The young man shrugs, nods, writes something down, seems to be arguing again. He smiles as he replaces the receiver.

He comes out and tells us that he has got us two seats on a plane this evening. I burst into tears.

It is hard for us to say good-bye. Uncles, aunts, nieces and nephews, cousins, grandmother. Seventeen people.

I remember a tiny pink and white gingham dress trimmed with white rickrack.

None of Walter's family survived Theresienstadt.

3

It is raining. The small airplane sits on the tarmac. In the canteen, people peer at it through the darkness. They drink coffee mixed with brandy. The loudspeaker makes them jump. They are nervous.

We are led out to the airplane. The pilot is separated from the passengers by a curtain. The engine outside my window spits fire into the rain. For a split second it lights up clouds, sheets of rain, a red circle around the propeller. Every one of the thirty uncomfortable seats is occupied. The passengers sit silently with their eyes closed. A young woman clenches her fists. A little girl clings to her father. Where is her mother? Are these people returning home, or are they refugees, forced to leave?

I sit there worrying. Will they let us in? Even with our visas, an English immigration officer has the right to refuse us entry.

We circle over London, a twinkling city.

Three immigration officers sit at three high desks, like lecterns. Do they sit so high to make us look up, to remind us of church, to make us tell the truth? They have the power to send us back. God is with me. He guides me to the officer on the right. I drop my passport, blush, grope for it on the floor, and hand it to him. He turns the pages, then looks at me. My nails cut into my palms.

"Where is your husband?" His voice is kind. I point at Walter.

"Call him over," he says. We stand in front of him together. "Why is your passport in the name of Miller?" he asks. I explain.

"You have a visa to enter this country on business. You are permitted to stay for fourteen days."

He examines Walter's passport.

"Your husband has a visitor's permit for three months. I will extend yours for the same amount of time."

I unclench my fists, straighten my back. The officer looks at me, concerned.

"How long do you wish to remain in England?" he asks.

"Forever," I reply innocently.

He smiles broadly. "You are only allowed to stay for three months," the officer says.

"Can't we apply for a longer stay?"

"Yes, but what will you do if you are refused? You can't go back to Austria."

"We'll have to try to go to America—Australia—South Africa—wherever will have us," Walter says in his broken English.

The officer stamps our passports with an entry visa for three months. "Good luck," he says, handing them to us.

We fetch our luggage and go to the arrivals hall, where Stefan, Walter's cousin, is waiting for us. He is small and slim, wears a navy blue suit. His blue-black hair and slanting eyes lend him a Japanese air.

We stand on English soil. I look at the wide, busy roads, the tall, impressive buildings, the orderly stream of traffic. I thank God.

We take a taxi to the Strand Palace Hotel. Stefan helps Walter with our luggage. He pays for our room for a night.

He says, "Uncle Paul brought me to England, too, and is letting me stay with him until I am settled. I have to do as he says. He wants me to let you know that business is bad, and that he has had heavy losses on the stock exchange. I don't believe it, but he doesn't want any further obligations."

I remember Prague.

* * *

There is a sharp knock at the door. Half-asleep, I sit up. *The Gestapo?* Walter jumps out of bed, opens the door. Early morning sun sneaks around the corner of a tall building. It is seven o'clock.

"Breakfast, sir." The waiter rolls in the table trolley, opens it up, pushes it between our beds, straightens the white linen tablecloth. I'm in a modern bedroom. Beige walls, carpets, and curtains. Two small chairs covered in orange tweed. A desk. Writing paper and envelopes. Advertising brochures. On my bedside table is a telephone and a Bible.

Walter is in the bathroom. "Hurry up," I call. "I'm starving."

Pretty pink flowers painted on white china. Butter, jam, marmalade, and rolls. Napkins, arranged like cones, stand at attention. There are two large plates covered with huge silver domes. I lift mine.

"Walter, an English breakfast! Bacon, eggs, tomatoes, mushrooms—hurry, it's getting cold!"

We drink coffee, eat, and talk all at once. I lie back to rest, to digest the huge meal and everything that has happened. Stefan is already waiting for us downstairs. He arranges for most of our luggage to be stored at the hotel until tomorrow. He is taking us to Kilburn to find us a room. I glance at the folded newspaper on the front desk: PEACE FOR OUR TIME, reads the headline.

4

It seems a long bus ride from the Strand to Kilburn. It is a warm, sunny autumn day. White clouds streak the blue sky. The air is fresher, cleaner than in Vienna. The bus crawls along the crowded Kilburn High Road. Mothers push prams, their small children holding on to them, eating apples. Window-shoppers drift. It is Saturday.

People look neat and clean. They seem to have money to spend. I have heard that two million people in England are unemployed, but maybe not in London?

A man sells flowers from a small cart. "Walter, look! English people queue for flowers!" I say. An old woman in a man's black felt hat is selling fruit.

The bus stops. Stefan takes us to a shop that sells newspapers, sweets, writing paper and envelopes, some paperback books. We look in the window and read the handwritten cards displayed there. A pram to sell. A boy's bicycle. Many of the cards read ROOM TO LET. Stefan notes down some addresses. He points out a large store.

"This is Woolworth's," he says. "Here you can buy nearly everything you need. They have only two prices: threepence and sixpence."

We arrive at the first address that Stefan has written down. The house is dilapidated, the windows dirty. I refuse to go inside. We walk to the next one. It looks somber. Stefan bangs the iron door knocker. A fat woman appears. Through the half-open door, I glimpse a dark hall, torn, dirty wallpaper, worn linoleum. She looks us up and down.

"Are you foreigners?" Her double chin quivers.

"Yes," I say quickly, and smile at her. She slams the door. I won't show Walter that I'm upset. We walk to Victoria Road, a side street off Kilburn High Road. It seems a friendly street, slightly wider than most, tidier, less noisy. I notice a low-built corner house. On a ground-floor window is a printed card: ROOM TO LET. There is a beautiful lime tree in the garden.

"Let's look at this one, Walter." I ring the bell. A withered old man opens the door. His toothless mouth and indrawn lips move up and down. Bright, friendly eyes question us.

"Is it about the room?" he peeps. We nod. "Come in." He opens the door wide. The walls in the hall are newly papered. There is a mirror. Some prints. A small, brightly colored rug lies on the stained, polished wooden floor. He takes us up to the top floor. I step through the door of a large, bright room. The sun shines through three clean windows. There is a large mahogany table and chairs. A huge cupboard stands against the off-white wall. I know we will be happy here. So does Walter.

"I have to charge fifteen shillings a week," the little man says. "There is a bathroom on the landing below. I'm afraid you'll have to pay threepence for each bath. Do you think that is too much?" He looks anxiously from Walter to me and back again.

"No, sir," Walter says. "We'd like to take it."

We give the landlord fifteen shillings and get in return two keys for the front door and two for our room.

"I hoped you would take it. I like to have young people in the house. I'm a widower; I live alone."

Stefan says good-bye; Uncle Paul is expecting him at home.

"Good luck to you both." He kisses me. "I'm sure you'll be happy here. Trudi, make him go to bed early. Tomorrow will be a hard day. I'll be over at eight in the morning. I've borrowed a handcart to collect your luggage."

When he is gone, Walter takes my arm. "Let's do some shopping—there's no food in the house."

Later on, after dinner, Walter is making coffee.

"Sit down," I say. "I want to talk to you."

"What about? Why are you looking so serious?"

"I don't want you to collect our luggage in a handcart."

"Why not?"

"I don't want you to do it. There's no need."

"How will we get it here otherwise, without it costing a fortune? We're refugees now. We've got no money. No income. I'm afraid you'll have to get used to it."

"We have no money, Walter, but we're not poor."

"We can't go to unnecessary expense." Walter's getting angry.

"We can charge my letters of credit," I argue. "Then we'll have some money, and you won't have to push a cart."

"Trudi, we have been through this. The money you have from Vienna is going into a bank account, where it will stay. Even if we have to live on bread and water. When your parents come, we will have to make a decent home for the four of us, and then we'll need it."

"I can't see what difference a few pounds will make."

"Oh, God, Trudi, a few pounds here, a few pounds there—soon there'll be nothing left. No. It can't be done."

"Look, Walter, I brought ten pounds in cash with me. We can use some of that, surely?"

"No. We need that money for living."

"It is just too much for you to drag that heavy cart. And it's degrading."

"Degrading? What are you talking about? It would be degrading to use your money, to pretend I'm still a gentleman of means. I'll take any job, do any work, but your money will stay in the bank."

Next morning, I am woken by the slam of the door to our room. Walter has gone. I rush to the window and look into the street; Walter and Stefan are pushing a cart toward Kilburn High Road.

"You are expected on Tuesday at seven o'clock for dinner," Stefan says. It sounds as though Uncle Paul is issuing an order rather than an invitation. He lives in a block of flats in St. John's Wood.

"Come in, come in," Stefan says. Uncle Paul is a tall, thin man of about fifty. We shake hands.

"Let me introduce you to Helen," he says, taking us into the sitting room. His girlfriend is a dumpy, middle-aged English lady. He shows us around the flat, then sits in a deep armchair, his long legs crossed. His dark hair is thick; his nose protrudes. He looks like a Tyrolean peasant. He shows Walter his golf trophies. I find it hard to make conversation with Helen. Stefan offers us sherry. Helen has cooked a simple dinner. Stefan serves the coffee and port.

"That was lovely, Helen, thank you," I say. She doesn't reply. I look at the mass-produced furniture, the loose covers, the faded curtains.

"How are you managing financially?" asks Uncle Paul.

"Trudi has some money. She also has her business allowance in letters of credit," Walter explains. "But there seems to be a hitch. She has to open a bank account before she can cash them, and we have been told that to do that she needs a reference from someone who lives here."

"That's correct." Uncle Paul laughs. "You can't go round opening bank accounts just like that!"

"Whyever not?"

"They like to know who they are dealing with."

"Ridiculous. It is *we* who need to know that. We are giving them our money. As Bernard Shaw said, 'The banker should provide the reference, since he is the one being trusted.' How does Trudi know they won't steal her money?"

"This is England! Such things don't happen here. However, Trudi"—he includes me in the conversation for the first time—"I have a better idea. Why don't you give *me* your money and let me put it into my account? I assure you it will be perfectly safe, and I can draw from it whenever you need money."

Walter winks at me.

"That is very kind of you, Uncle Paul, but we couldn't possibly put you to that kind of trouble every time we need money."

"Uncle, can't you recommend Trudi to your own bank manager so she can open an account there?" Walter asks.

"Well . . . er . . . yes . . . why not? I daresay that might be arranged."

"Shall we go in the morning?"

"No, I'm afraid that's out of the question. I'm busy all week, I'm afraid." He gazes at the carpet.

We go into the sitting room. Uncle Paul looks annoyed.

"I want to thank you for helping Walter," I say. "Do you realize that you saved his life? Bless you." He doesn't reply.

"Our country is doing a fine job," he says. "We're taking in all these penniless people without knowing anything about them or their backgrounds. As if we haven't enough unemployment! Now there'll be more mouths to feed. They are not permitted to work, and we taxpayers will have to keep them. They should be grateful to everyone in this country. They should never for a moment forget that they are allowed to be here only by the grace of our king and country. They should behave accordingly. Isn't that so, Helen?"

"Quite right, darling." She sounds disgusted. "But they *are* foreigners. Present company excepted, of course."

The last bus home is our excuse to leave. The good-byes are cool.

Stefan sees us to the bus stop. "You must forgive them," he says. "They're ignorant. They're not really bad people." I like Stefan.

I am very upset when we get home. Walter tries to cheer me up.

"Don't take any notice. Paul's a has-been who never was. Just because he's naturalized, he imagines he's English. Pompous old goat."

"No one will let us forget that we are foreigners!" I shout. "It's a dirty word!"

"Look, darling, for anyone coming to England, the first year is bound to be hard."

"Hard? It's impossible! Everything is so difficult! I speak English, but I can't understand even the newspaper headlines. I can't understand the advertisements on the Underground. The money confuses me. An English shilling is twelve pence, not ten, like in Austria. I can't do the calculations."

"You're taking things too seriously."

I shake my head. "How was I to know we were overstaying our welcome? And I didn't know it's rude to pay a compliment. When I praised Helen's cooking, she pretended not to hear. English people are so cold!"

"Not cold, darling. Reserved."

"I nearly cried when I mentioned my parents, and I don't

understand why I should hide the fact that I'm unhappy. It's absurd!"

"Sssh. You're getting hysterical."

"Don't shush me! I am so unhappy. When someone bumps into me on the pavement, I feel as though I should go down on my knees to apologize. I'm in *his* country. It's *his* pavement, it's *his* right-of-way. I'm only *allowed* to be here, I have no actual *rights*. Walter, I can't live like this."

Walter takes me to the Kilburn State Cinema, the largest cinema in Europe. We watch a depressing film about slaves in the American South. Black men are taken away from their families; women and children working in the fields are whipped. They have no rights at all. I am terribly upset. When the lights go up, there is music, and everyone stands up straight.

"What's going on?" I ask Walter.

He puts a finger to his lips and whispers, "It's the national anthem."

I remember Uncle Paul's words about king and country. I whisper, "I want to thank you very much, King George, for letting us come to England." I don't move. I hardly dare breathe. I stand tall, full of respect and gratitude. Tears roll down my cheeks.

"Why were you crying?" Walter asks me on the way back to Victoria Road.

"I want to go home."

5

Walter won't be back for hours. I slip back under the blankets. On the wall opposite is a gas fire. You have to put a shilling in the slot to switch it on. I look around the room—it will be expensive to heat a large space like this, up in the roof. But I know that I can earn money. I have contacts in London and a good reputation in the millinery trade—and Viennese designers have a certain cachet.

I am very worried about my parents. There is so much to do.

Today I have an appointment with Lady Gertrude Balfour, who is the sister of Montagu Norman, the governor of the Bank of England. She has just come down to London from her house in Scotland. Nemone, her daughter, studied singing in Vienna; she was my customer, and we became friends. I met her mother when Nemone brought her to the salon. I telephoned Lady Balfour because I thought she might be able to help with visas for my parents.

I stand in front of a small, white Georgian house in Grosvenor Street, Mayfair. The front door is highly polished. The brass door handle, knocker, and bellpull shine. There are coach lamps on each side of the entrance.

"Mrs. Ehrlich? You are expected."

The butler leads me through a spacious hall into a large sitting room. Tall and slim, her white hair piled up on her head, Lady Balfour hasn't changed since I last saw her in Vienna.

"Nemone is worried about you. She is in New York at the moment. It must have been very hard for you. If you don't want to talk about it, my dear, I quite understand."

Nevertheless I tell her about what happened to us in Vienna, about how Walter was persecuted, and about the lengths we had to go to in order to get him a visa.

"And what about your parents?" she asks.

"Can you help me bring them to England? Please? I can support them myself—your guarantee would be just a formality."

She tells me that she will speak to her husband about it. The butler serves fresh haddock roe, rolled in flour and fried, garnished with sliced, pickled cucumbers.

"I hope you like our Scottish food," Lady Balfour says.

I think of Walter and my goulash.

The room is flooded with sunlight, leaves rustle against the windows, silk taffeta curtains shimmer. Fine old furniture, emerald green satin-covered sofa, pink roses, oil paintings, the butler in his dark suit and white shirt. And my parents are in Vienna, in danger.

I can't sleep at night, waiting to hear from Lady Balfour. I dream that my parents are looking at me through barbed wire, pressing their faces against it. They call me: "Truderl!" I wake up screaming.

Two days later, I find a letter on the hall table. It is addressed, *To my daughter, 84 Victoria Road, London, England.* My mother's handwriting. She was afraid even to write my name.

15 October 1938

Darling,

We are both well and miss you very much. We received your letter. Don't worry, we can manage with the money we have. All we want is to embrace our daughter again. Father sends his love and joins me in my wish.

All our love,

Mother

A letter arrives from Scotland. Lady Balfour writes that she is willing to give a guarantee for my father, but not for my mother; the responsibility for two old people would be too much. I would have to find someone else to do it.

"Isn't it mean, not to give a guarantee for both of them?" Walter asks.

"No, darling, not mean, just cautious. Scottish people are careful with money. We'll find something for Mother. I'm just grateful for Lady Balfour's help with Father."

A few days later, I get another letter, one that makes me cry as I read it:

18 October 1938

Dear Madame,

It is now three months since my lady went to England on a selling trip. I have not heard from her, and I have the feeling that she will not return.

I have kept the business going as well as I could, but without her it isn't the business it was. Customers are asking for her, the girls are upset, and now is the time to go to Paris for the spring collections. I cannot do this. I know nothing about Paris, I have no money, and I am not a designer.

I had to close the business and hand the key to the Gestapo. It was a hard decision to make, and a hard thing to do. I did everything the way my lady would have wanted me to. She wasn't a boss. She was our friend—and we miss her.

I had just enough money left to pay the girls. There was enough left over to buy cakes. We made coffee and sat in the workroom, reminiscing about our lovely times together, and we cried. We wished our Madame good luck. And then we sang:

Muas i denn, muas i denn, zum Städtle hinaus,
Städtle hinaus und Du mein Schatz bleibst hier.
Wann i kum, wann i kum, wann i wieder, wieder kum,
Wieder, wieder kum, kehr ich ein mein Schatz bei Dir.
Kann i gleich net immer bei Dir sein,
Han i doch mein Herzele bei Dir.
Wann i kum, wann i kum, wann i wieder wieder kum,
Wieder, wieder kum, kehr ich ein mein Schatz bei Dir.

(Do I have to, do I have to leave my town?
When you, my dear, stay here?
When I come, when I come, when I come back again,
I will come to you, my dear.
I can't always be at your side,
But I left my heart with you.
When I come, when I come, when I come back again,
Back I will come to you, my dear.)

Madame, I wrote all the lines of the song so you won't forget them. Not forgetting them, is not forgetting us.
Yours respectfully,
Steffi

I hear about a millinery firm in the West End run by two German brothers, refugees from Frankfurt, Otto and Fritz Levy. I telephone and make an appointment to see them. I put on my smart, blue tweed suit.

"It suits you," says Walter. "You look respectable."

"I'm going to the West End to apply for a job as a designer. I need to look chic, not respectable."

I catch the number 8 bus to Marble Arch and hurry down Oxford Street. Crossing the road, I find myself standing in front of Waring and Gillow, a furniture store. The Clarendon Hat Company is on the third floor of a building around the corner.

I walk through a large workroom. Girls bend over their worktables, looking up at me with narrowed eyes—watching the rabbit. The young German forelady, stocky, blond, blue-eyed, sits at a separate table, dipping sugared biscuits into coffee. She pretends not to notice me. The afternoon sun casts four elongated shadow table legs across the floor. The room is sober. I think of my workroom in Vienna, my girls, my Steffi, straws, silks, velvets, flowers, feathers, and veiling: the glitter of it all.

I am asked to take a seat. The workroom buzzes. These girls are going to be dancers, nurses, secretaries—anything but milliners. My tweed jacket feels hot and scratchy. My mouth is dry.

I am introduced to the brothers Levy. They are alike, yet so different. Otto Levy, who runs the factory in Luton, is the older one. He is losing his hair. Fritz, the one who might be my boss, is dark-haired with clever, cynical, olive black eyes. His teeth are strong and white. They ask me a lot of questions. They tell me the German designer is going home to be married; she wants to leave before war breaks out.

"Do you know Paris well?" Otto asks.

"Very well," I reply.

They look at each other. "We will be in touch."

At four o'clock, depressed and thirsty, I cross Oxford Street again, cursing everything to do with the hat business.

Walter is out. I take off my suit, kick off the smart, tight shoes, and put on my dressing gown. From across the backyard, I can hear the clatter of pots and pans. People shout, children scream. I dream of Paris.

Three days later, Walter stands at the door waving a letter.

THE CLARENDON HAT COMPANY, OXFORD STREET, LONDON is printed on the envelope.

"They want me! Hooray!"

We buy a bottle of wine to celebrate, drinking it in bed, in each other's arms.

I wake late the next morning. Walter has already been out. He brings me a tray with coffee, fresh rolls, butter, and jam. One red rose. In spite of all the worry about our people in Vienna, I have never been so happy. I look around the room—our home. I love the peculiar curtains, the washbasin, stove, and cooking utensils concealed behind a gray curtain, the dining table and chairs. I even love the umbrella in the corner, waiting to protect us from the leaking roof above our bed.

Sometimes I get a bit hysterical. I shout at Walter, but the next moment I want to hold him, stroke his hair, kiss him. He knows. He looks at me, head cocked to one side, and grins.

A letter arrived from the Home Office. They were granting me a permit to work as a designer for the Clarendon Hat Company. And my permit for a three-month stay in England had been canceled; I was now a permanent resident.

"Walter! I don't understand—maybe it's a mistake? I thought foreigners had to be in England for three years to apply for permanent residence, and five years for naturalization. I have been here for four weeks—and I haven't applied for anything. How did I get it?"

"It's wonderful," says Walter. "Why worry?"

"But darling, we need a permit for you as well—one is no good."

The Levys recommend a solicitor in the City. We sit in a mahogany-paneled office, in front of a large mahogany desk. A red and blue Persian rug beneath our feet. Hundreds of books line the wall. We are waiting, sitting in two comfortable leather armchairs. The leather is old, and the top layer is temptingly easy to peel off. Walter gives me a reproving look, and I stop.

When the lawyer arrives, I hand him my letter from the Home Office. "Well?" He gives me a questioning look. He has clear hazel eyes.

"How did I get this permit? I didn't even apply for it."

"When you arrived in this country, did the immigration officer ask you how long you wished to remain in England?"

"Yes. I told him we wanted to stay forever."

His expression is the same as the one on the immigration officer's face when he heard my reply.

"There's your answer. You told him the truth. Knowing you wanted to stay forever, he allowed you in, and that became what is called your landing condition."

"Will you take us on as your clients?" I ask.

"With pleasure. What can I do for you?"

"Can you get the same permit for my husband?"

Six weeks later, Walter was granted permission to stay in England permanently.

"Walter, *now* do you believe in miracles?"

He laughs. "No."

* * *

We have met some other Viennese émigrés, and we decide to have a dinner party for them. I try to make our room pretty; I want Walter to be proud of it. I try to drape the ugly cotton curtains to break up their design of purple flowers. Behind the gray curtain in the corner, in our "kitchen," are three tall, gaudily decorated ceramic Victorian vases. I put them on the three window ledges, turning them plain-side out. I fill them with green leaves and yellow chrysanthemums.

I have a huge, yellow silk shawl with a yellow silk fringe that I used to wear with a black silk sheath; now it does duty as a bedspread. The brown furniture, the brown linoleum, even the purple flowered curtains don't look too bad now.

Walter arrives home with onions, potatoes, and apples. He is delighted when he sees what I have done. "You're a genius," he says, dropping the shopping bag and waltzing me around the room until I'm breathless.

At Woolworth's, we hunt down reject plates and glasses and search the stalls for oddments of cutlery. Walter sees a small glass vase. It is slightly chipped, but he can't resist it. "Darling, it is only sixpence and it'll look nice on the table." He feels guilty because he knows I can't bear things that are chipped or cracked.

I make goulash. The meat costs four pence a pound. My mother taught me to use the same weight of onions as meat. Walter peels potatoes. It is raining.

"Four pounds of potatoes for a penny!" Walter says. "Who's coming?"

"Mitzi and her new business partner, Esther. Pepi's friend Jacobi—he's fat and clever and plays bridge for a living."

"Lucky fellow. Who else?"

"Adrian—the one with money in America. He carefully pulls up his trouser knees before he sits down, inspects his food minutely with a fork before eating, refolds the newspaper after reading it. And he's a bit of a snob."

"So why did you ask him?"

"Well—he's nice, and good-looking, and he's got class."

"Do you flirt with him?" Walter comes up behind me and puts his arms around me. I drop the wooden spoon, full of gravy. He has to mop it up.

Egg mayonnaise on a bed of crisp lettuce and watercress is already on the table. Walter switches on the overhead light; its enormous yellow paper shade throws a warm glow onto the table, putting it center stage. Walter was right. The glass vase, filled with blue flowers, looks pretty next to the green lettuce, the yellow and white eggs. The odd pieces of cutlery gleam. White paper napkins stand upright in water glasses. I look around the cozy room. In this light, even the peculiar curtains look nice.

Oh, Walter, remember how proud we were?

"We have a home again," Walter said, and kissed me.

Out of the corner of my eye, I see the apples he has bought. "Look at those horrible things!" I shout at him. "They are supposed to be our dessert!"

"Darling, they were the cheapest I could find—"

"They look it," I cut him off.

My old friend Mitzi is the first to arrive. Her appraising eyes flash about the room.

"Can't you close the windows?" she complains. "It's freezing in here."

She is wearing a light blue wool coatdress which matches her eyes. Her hair is soft, blond. I haven't put on a good dress because I didn't want to get goulash on it; now I feel like the cook.

Adrian arrives: gray flannel suit, red bow tie. Mitzi stops talking midsentence and stares at him, mouth hanging open. She goes over to introduce herself—she is short and has to put her head back to look up at him—and from that moment on she doesn't leave his side.

In the kitchen corner of the room, Walter hisses at me, "She's horrible—why did you have to invite her?"

"Oh, she only saved our lives, darling, that's all."

Adrian perches on the edge of our divan bed, on my yellow silk shawl. Mitzi positions herself next to him, firing questions at him.

Esther and Jacobi arrive together, having been caught in the rain. He runs his fingers through his unkempt red hair. Esther is wearing a navy blue suit. Her reedlike body moves gracefully. I introduce her to Adrian.

"Delicious smell," Jacobi says, sniffing appreciatively. "Is it goulash?"

"Dinner is served," I announce.

Our guests help themselves to the egg mayonnaise, and then I go to the "kitchen" to serve the goulash. Esther gets up and follows me, offering to help. Adrian's brown eyes are fixed on her long, beautiful legs. So are Walter's. He pours beer for our guests. They chat and laugh. They eat and drink. Esther's eyes seek out Walter's.

"Have you heard from Pepi?" Jacobi asks me.

"Yes—and I'm very worried. They've lost his permit at the American consulate. He's trying to come to England—his girlfriend, Gina, came with a domestic permit, and she's been here to ask my advice."

"What's she like?" Mitzi asks.

"Fair hair, blue eyes. He's quite serious about her. Of course"—I look at Walter—"she's not as beautiful as Esther. Gina has applied for him to come over with some kind of youth organization, but of course he's far too old; she's given a false date of birth. I wish he had asked my advice earlier. If he's found out, and they cancel his permit, he will never be allowed in again. You know the English."

"Are you still planning to go to America?" Walter asks Jacobi.

"I'll have to. I'd much rather stay here, but my wife is there already; I'm just waiting for my visa."

"What about you?" I ask Adrian. "You have a sister in New York, don't you?"

"I have an American visa and could go whenever I want, but I prefer it here." Suddenly I feel sorry for him. He is thirty-six, and on his own.

"I'm staying here, too," says Mitzi, batting her eyelashes at him. "Why do you prefer it?"

"Inertia," replies Adrian. "I enjoy being a man of leisure in London."

"Have you ever worked?" Mitzi asks.

Adrian looks uncomfortable. "There's work and work, Mitzi," he says enigmatically.

"Adrian believes in money and power," I say. "His sister sends him a monthly allowance from America. He doesn't have to lift a finger."

"I should be so lucky," Jacobi sighs.

The men start to talk about politics.

"When Churchill demanded that Britain rearm, Chamberlain refused. What a mess! *Now* they start air-raid precautions and gas masks! *Now* they are digging trenches in the parks! A bit late, isn't it?" Jacobi says.

"The navy and the air force have been mobilized," Walter observes.

Adrian laughs. "We never hear about the army, though. Is there one?"

"Don't be so cynical," says Walter. "I'm sure the English know what they're doing."

"Chamberlain meets Hitler and comes home with an agreement selling out Czechoslovakia—and you say they know what they're doing! Peace with honor! Peace for our time! Chamberlain must be mad." Adrian bangs the table.

"Churchill called it a shameful betrayal. He's angry—the whole country's angry," Jacobi says.

Everyone has had second helpings and plenty of beer. We have eaten the apples and drunk coffee. Adrian makes his excuses and says a special good-bye to Esther. When he kisses her hand, her amber eyes follow Walter to the door, where he waits to see Adrian out.

As soon as he has left, everyone starts talking about him. They don't much like him, but once he has gone, it's as though the evening's focus has disappeared. It's always like that with Adrian. The others start saying good-bye and getting ready to go. "Come again," I say to everyone except Esther.

Once they have all gone, Walter opens the windows and clears up. My yellow shawl hangs over the back of a chair. I go downstairs to the bathroom, then come back up and get into bed, turning my face to the wall and pulling the blanket right up over my head. Walter gets into his pajamas but sits at the table. He doesn't say anything. I wait. My temples are throbbing. I feel sick. I get up and take two aspirin. He doesn't look up, just stares down at the table. I can't contain myself.

"Can't you even apologize?" I ask.

He doesn't answer.

"Can you hear me? I'm talking to you!" I shout. I hurl the yellow shawl onto the floor. "How could you do this to me? In front of all the others!"

"Do *what*, exactly?" Walter's voice is hard.

"Flirt with Esther," I say, "so blatantly. How could you *do* this to me?" I'm howling now. "I can't help it if she's more beautiful than I am!"

"She isn't." Walter shakes his head slowly.

I wipe my face with the back of my hand. Walter gets up and dries my tears with his handkerchief.

"I've done nothing wrong, darling. I know she tried. But she didn't succeed, and I made sure that she knew it."

"Now you want *me* to apologize?"

"Come to bed, darling," he whispers.

6

After many delays and lost documents and weeks of anxious waiting in Vienna, Walter's brother-in-law Hans and his wife Gretl get visas for England. When they arrive, they are sad and quiet. They cling to each other, and to Peter, their four-year-old son. Gretl has a job as a cook-housekeeper for a family in the countryside outside London; Peter will be able to go with her. She doesn't want to leave. Her eyes are frightened.

Hans is telling us about what happened in Vienna.

"The knock at the door wasn't a request for admission—it was a demand," he says. He looks out of the window, blinking rapidly. "I knew I had to open the door, but I didn't expect to be kicked into the room."

His hair, eyebrows, and lashes are white-blond. His pale blue eyes are half-covered by his pink eyelids, as if they cannot bear the light.

"Don't talk about it if it upsets you," I say.

"There isn't much to tell. Everybody knows what they do behind closed doors. They asked where my money was hidden. Gretl's jewels. 'We have none,' I told them. 'We're not rich.' One of them went into the cloakroom. The one in charge told me to get my coat, that I had to go with them to Gestapo headquarters. Gretl was screaming. Suddenly, Peter appeared from under the piano. He put his little arms around the man's leg. 'He is my papi,' he said. 'Don't take him away. Please!' Then he put his head against the man's thigh and kissed it. 'Please, Herr Nazi, don't take him away. Please.' The German came right up to me. 'Get yourself to the town cemetery,' he whispered. 'Quick. Now. Stay there until midday tomorrow.' I left there and then, and ran without stopping, faster than I have ever run in my life." Hans stares into space. "I owe that Nazi my life. He must have a boy of Peter's age." A smile splits his face.

7

8 November 1938

Dear Mother,

When I write to you, I feel like a little girl again, the little girl who called you Mama.

I'm so glad Steffi brings my letters to you. It's good to know that you and Father are well. If you need any help, please ask her. She is very loyal. If you need money, she'll write to me, and I will send it at once. I miss her so much, especially now that I have a job as a designer in a small hat salon near Bond Street. It's in a similar position to mine at Kohlmarkt, but nothing else is the same. It's not as bright or sunny, or as nicely furnished. The milliners aren't my girls. There's no Steffi, and I can't telephone Mama whenever I want. They pay me £1 a week—I don't have a work permit yet. And they have paid for my collection of model hats to be released by customs, and they're going to help me sell them. 150 hats should bring in a lot of money. A fortune, in our present position. I will use it to make a nice home for all of us.

I am waiting to hear from the Home Office about your visas. It won't be long, Mother, don't worry.

Here we have the coldest of cold dawns, turning into warm autumn weather during the day. Walter is my mother and father, brother and sister; he is my child. We are happy in

our large, bright room in the eaves. The days and nights slip
away. Some mornings, when I'm half-asleep, I stretch out my
hand to make certain that he is still here.

   I love you both.
      Trudi

My collection of model hats had finally been released by customs and was to be sold at Barbara's Hat Salon, a place near
the Clarendon Hat Company with flock wallpaper, mirrors
in carved gilt frames, large oil paintings, red velvet curtains,
and mahogany furniture. The business belonged to Barbara
and her associate Valerie.

They helped me to unpack the hats. They made me try
them on, talk about them, explain how they were made—a
kind of sales pitch.

Valerie's face is flushed, and her ginger hair falls over her
freckled face. Barbara is calm, her black eyes amused. They
gush over my hats; I'm embarrassed by their praise. Barbara
suggests that we stage a show for select customers.

Next morning, she flies into the workroom from the
salon, eyes ablaze. "Help, Trudi, you've got to help me. She's
impossible. Nothing's ever right for her. She's well past it, the
fat, ugly cow. She puts the sailor cap with hanging ribbons on
her big head—she looks like one of the three little pigs—and
announces she wants to buy it! You deal with her; I can't."

"Who is she?" I ask.

"A rich widow who thinks she's eighteen. She's man crazy.
Her boyfriend just did a runner."

The lady—tall, square, without a waist—stands like a tree trunk in front of a showcase. She pulls out one hat after another, throws them onto the table, drops them on the floor. She catches one of her high heels in some veiling, totters, and nearly falls. Valerie shrugs, looks over at me apologetically. She's near tears.

I say, "Good morning, madame. May I help you?" She does not reply, just picks up her gold-rimmed lorgnette and looks past me. She picks up my large black velour beret. Her clumsy fingers prod and poke. She sails to the mirror, sits down, and plonks the beret on her iron gray hair.

"Put some veiling on it," she orders, without glancing at me. "I hope you can understand English—I never know with you foreigners."

Valerie shoots me a worried glance. I bring over some finemeshed veiling, arrange it carefully, and tie it into a neat bow at the back of the hat. I don't care if it looks good or not, but for the sake of Valerie and Barbara, I say in my most subdued, respectful voice, "Madame, it looks beautiful at your backside."

She stiffens. Her eyes stab me. Valerie runs out of the room, apparently choking. Barbara's hand is covering her mouth. I realize what I have said, and blush.

For the hat show, customers arrive in chauffeur-driven limousines wearing Balenciaga and Patou, jewelry from Van Cleef & Arpels and Cartier, sables, mink, chinchilla. They push and shove to get the best seats. White mink on black suits. Russian lynx on a red coat. Pearls. Diamonds.

The crystal drops hanging from the gilt chandelier shoot sharp lines across the Persian carpet. The salon is filled with pink flowers. Pink hats draped with pink chiffon squares are arranged in the showcase. Every seat is taken. People lean against walls, holding glasses of champagne. Women chat, smile, say hello.

Barbara and Valerie are beaming. Valerie nudges me and giggles. "Look at the Adonis standing behind the baroness. He's a gigolo." Valerie is wearing a white, tailored tweed suit, a huge cabochon emerald on a string of pearls around her neck. She's the best-dressed woman in the room.

We begin. From the workroom, where I am pinning up my hair, I hear Barbara announce, "Ladies and gentlemen, we are proud to present a collection of hats designed by Mrs. Trudi Ehrlich, who has brought them here from Vienna. She has kindly agreed to model three of her designs for you. We hope you will be as enchanted as we were." Applause.

I am wearing a short, sleeveless, black crepe de chine shift with a large diamanté clip at my shoulder. I put the black ostrich feather toque on; it fits as closely as a wig. An ostrich fringe falls onto each cheek, covers my forehead. I glance in the mirror. My heart is pounding. I have seen Paris fashion shows, mannequins floating as if on a cloud, trailing long chiffon scarves. I know what to do, but I'm nervous. I walk around the room, turning to display the hat from all angles.

Back in the workroom, I put on a tiny, pink, draped chiffon pillbox, tilt it slightly forward, and arrange the long ends of the draping around my neck. I am more confident this time. The women's eyes are shining. Then comes the pièce de résistance: a black broadtail model with a large brim and a diamanté band around the flat crown. I wear it with long, pink suede gloves.

"Bravo, madame, bravo," shouts the gigolo.

We bring in the hats. The scrum begins. Vixens fight for their prey. A diamond bracelet catches in veiling. Sharp red nails crush velvet. A mascaraed lynx glares at another.

"My hats, my lovely hats, what are you doing to them?"

In the scrum, I step on the foot of the baroness, who screams. Her open mouth shows perfect teeth smeared with lipstick. Are these wild creatures the same ladies who arrived in limousines? I see Valerie's terrified face. The gigolo is leaning against a wall, laughing. The women know they have to buy now—the models are one-offs. I see them leave clutching several hats. We have to bring in more and more from the back room. Ladies are trying on hats in the bathroom.

We serve customers until late in the evening. By the end, only a few hats are left—Barbara wants to keep them to take orders. I am happy and exhausted—and astonished. Yes, they were lovely hats. But not *that* lovely.

I walk up New Bond Street. The wind buffets me around the corner into Oxford Street. Rain dims the streetlights, ships against shopwindows. I stop at Bond Street Station to buy a newspaper. "Not a good night," the newspaper man greets me. I can see people stopping to read his placard; I try to get near it to read it myself: POGROM IN VIENNA.

I grab the newspaper.

Pogrom . . . bombs . . . synagogues . . . explosions . . . thousands of Jews arrested. From our Vienna correspondent, 10 November 1938.

My shaking hands drop my purse. Coins roll off the curb. I wait at the bus stop, the newspaper inside my coat to protect it from the rain. I don't want to read it, not without Walter. I hurry along Victoria Road, shaking.

Walter isn't home yet. I take off my wet clothes, change into my warm dressing gown, and pace back and forth with bare feet, shivering. The newspaper lies on the table. I see young Brownshirts in my parents' house. Father stands in front of Mother, his hands outstretched. He says calmly to one of them, "Young man, my wife is not Jewish. Leave her alone." They laugh.

I feel so guilty. Their applications are sitting at the Home Office while I wait for a reply. I'll go first thing in the morning; I'll sit in the corridor and wait until I have permission to bring my parents to England. I will not move until I get it.

I hear the front door close, Walter coming up the stairs. He sees me, by now huddled on the floor. He sits down next to me, still wearing his wet overcoat and hat. He holds me, lets me cry.

"What's happened, darling?" he asks.

I point to the newspaper. His eyelids crease as he reads the headline.

He puts me to bed and gives me a cup of tea and a small brandy. He says this pogrom is the German's revenge for the shooting of a German diplomat by a Polish Jew in Paris two days ago. He reads me some of the newspaper report: "Anti-Jewish rioting broke out shortly after midnight. Jewish shops were attacked by crowds incited by Brownshirts, windows smashed, goods destroyed or looted. The second-largest synagogue in Vienna has been destroyed by a bomb."

"Walter, I don't care about buildings—I care about people, about my family, your family, the Millers!"

Walter tries to reassure me—my parents live on the second floor of an old building in a quiet neighborhood. He tells me not to panic. Eventually, he falls asleep. I sit at the window, looking at the moon.

Next morning, Walter comes up the stairs waving a telegram.

ALL IS WELL STOP FANNY

I laugh and cry. Steffi, my friend Stefanie: sometimes we used to call her Fanny.

8

11 November 1938: it was a stampede at the Home Office. Hundreds of people were milling around, anxious for news of relatives and friends, and not only in Austria and Germany; the pogrom had frightened Jews in Czechoslovakia, Poland, Holland, France, and Italy. Applications for British visas flooded every desk.

Once more I stand in a long queue in front of an official building, not knowing how to get inside. This time there is no kindly taxi driver to help me. I pull my coat tightly around me and wait for two hours, then hurry home, longing for warmth. I'm depressed about my parents. They are alone and frightened. What can I do to help them? My feet are too cold for inspiration. I go to bed.

I remember my mother coming to say good night to me before she and my father go out in the evening. She wears her favorite marquise-cut ruby ring. Surrounded by diamonds, the bloodred stone sparkles. She tells me it came from the Czar's collection. In her wine-colored chiffon dress, golden hair piled high, she is a fairy queen, Father her handsome prince. They cuddle and hold hands; they're in love. They go out; I stay with Marie.

All day, Father is in his workroom. Mother cooks, sends Marie shopping. Mother goes out to meet friends. I run to

Marie in the kitchen. They buy me lovely toys, but they never play with me.

I can't bear to think of my parents in danger. I want to go back to rescue them.

"All you can do is wait," says Walter, turning on the lights. He sits on the bed, smoking, gazing out of the window. Sheets of sleet cling to the glass.

Every morning I queue at the Home Office. After several days, the queues shorten. I am directed to the clerk in charge of my parents' case. He can't find their file, promises to telephone the next day, doesn't. I telephone the Home Office. The line is engaged. I go back and queue. Lady Balfour's letter has been lost. I manage to get her to write another one. I queue again in the snow. And so it goes, on and on.

My mother writes, "You don't care about us. We can't stay here any longer. We're going to Shanghai."

"That's unfair!" Walter is angry. "They know how reliable you are."

They are desperate.

I don't hear from Mother. I'm extremely worried. I take the chance and ring Vienna.

"Mother! How are you?"

"We're fine." Mother's voice is faint.

"I can't hear you properly. Is Father there?"

"He's out."

"Mother, for goodness' sake, what's the matter?"

"Nothing, darling, we're fine."

"Mother, we're doing all we can . . ."

Much later, I learn that Steffi had asked my parents regularly if they needed money. The answer was always the same: "No, no, Trudi left us plenty. If we need anything, we will tell you." The fact was that they had been robbed of almost everything and were penniless. They were selling what was left of their possessions, one by one. Eventually, all that was left was the bedroom suite and Mother's marquise ring. Father pawned the ring, hoping to sell the bedroom suite when they left Vienna and use the money to redeem it. But the redemption date came and went, the pawnbroker sold the ring on, and Father had to sell the bedroom suite straightaway in order to get it back. On the day I telephoned, Father was lying on a mattress on the floor, in an empty house, dangerously ill.

The Jewish doctor who had examined my father told my mother that he had a blocked bowel. She was instructed to give him three tablespoons of castor oil every six hours. If this didn't open the bowel, surgery was the only option, and the chance of success was small. That night, my mother's boldness and pluck returned. She gave him seven tablespoons of castor oil. And the miracle happened. He recovered.

They had to sell the ring.

At Christmas, Walter and I walk arm in arm along Oxford Street. Rain or no rain, the streets are packed with shoppers. Unemployed or not, people are buying. I remember Vienna: the exquisite window displays, the pretty, sparkling lights. There, Christmas was a religious affair. People went to church, had a meal with family, drank a glass of wine, watched children's excited faces as they opened their presents. Here, people with fraught expressions snatch glass and pottery out of each other's hands. The shops are in chaos. Customers are "served" by people recruited specially for the season. I ask to see some Waterford glass and get only a disdainful look.

"Do you remember how cold it was last year?" I ask Walter. It was the only time I could remember him wearing his father's coat—black, nutria-lined, with a Spitzbieber collar. "That coat made you look so rich."

Walter laughs loudly.

I wonder what my parents are doing.

I had managed to save seven shillings and sixpence to buy a Parker cigarette lighter for Walter, my first present to him in England. It made my Christmas.

9

I go to Barbara's Hat Salon to collect payment for my hats. "We're so sorry you can't stay on here," Valerie says. Barbara nodded in agreement. I was sorry, too. And hurt, and bitter. The money they paid me for my collection of hats was half of what I was entitled to. I knew how much they had charged their customers, and even with the import duty, they had made an enormous profit. What they paid me didn't even cover my costs in Vienna. And my collection had lifted them into the first rank of milliners.

They gave me a check and took me through Bond Street, across Oxford Street to Vere Street, and into Barclays Bank. Barbara introduced me to the manager, a corpulent man with a damp handshake. We exchanged a few words, I signed a form, and I left, the proud owner of a bank account with one of the biggest banks in England. I thanked Valerie and Barbara, said good-bye, and never went to see them again.

Next morning at nine, I am to start at the Clarendon Hat Company as head designer. When Walter brings me breakfast in bed, I say, yawning, "I don't mind working late at night, but I hate getting up early."

"It's all about the time of day you were born. It must have been late at night when you stuck your little nose into the world." He laughs. "Come on, you lazy thing, you have to be on time. This is a real job."

"What are you going to do today?"

"I'll do some shopping: meat for dinner, a tin of fruit. We need milk. Then I'll go to the Gaumont. For sixpence, I can sit through as many performances as I like. That way, I'm saving money for the gas meter and learning English at the same time."

I walk to the bus stop in the High Road; the cold morning air stings my cheeks and makes my eyes smart.

Clothes in the shopwindows are brown, tan, and gorse

green. I admire a smart petrol-blue pullover with a roll-neck. It would suit Walter. Nightdresses have changed from pale blue and pink cotton to red and blue floral flannel.

The flower seller in the street has gone. The woman at her fruit cart wears knitted gloves, one gray, one black. She has cut off the fingertips so that she can handle money quickly. A strong breeze blows across a sky streaked with dark, racing clouds. I take my place in the queue at the bus stop. A middle-aged man stands in front of me. He wears a gray felt hat, creased raincoat, and shoes that haven't seen polish for a long time. A fat pipe sticks to his lip. Three chirpy young girls are rubbing their gloveless hands together. They giggle as the wind ruffles their skirts, blows brown and blond hair across their cheeks. I clutch my hat and glance at my reflection in an optician's window. In this unkind light, my hair burns as red as fire beneath the small-brimmed brown felt. I look like a schoolmistress. The man in front of me removes his pipe from his mouth, spits, and puts it back again.

Our bus arrives. It is half past eight.

I remember everything about that morning. A new chapter has begun. I am no longer my own boss. For the first time, I am an employee. Yet I feel happy and proud. I feel as though I have joined a club. A club of people who travel to work together, early in the morning. People who have jobs. These are chosen people, and I am one of them.

I arrive at the Clarendon Hat Company and, remembering my reflection in the optician's window, take off my hat and let my hair loose.

A young, uniformed porter opens the lift door and takes me up to the third floor. I walk into the workroom of the Clarendon Hat Company, cool, upright, at five minutes to nine.

"Good morning, ladies," I say. There should be eighteen milliners, but only half of them have arrived. I notice Belinda, the assistant designer, is sitting in the designer's chair, at the designer's table—*my* chair, *my* table—her nose buried in papers. She doesn't look up.

"Good morning, Belinda," I say loudly as I walk past. "Be so kind as to clear my table of Miss Stradler's belongings, and your own. And please change that chair—I prefer an armchair." She blushes crimson.

I stalk through the glass doors into the office. "Good morning," I greet Gwen and Alice, the secretaries. They glance up and mutter, "Good morning, miss," before returning to their files.

I take off my brown mackintosh and walk over to my desk. I can see them following me with hostile eyes; when I look across at them, they quickly busy themselves with their work.

I put a photograph of Walter and one of my parents on my desk, with a small vase containing three pink chrysanthemums. Alice jumps up to fetch some water for them.

I return to the workroom. It lacks glamour, excitement. How I miss Steffi. But Belinda has carried out her instructions.

Fritz Levy comes in at ten o'clock, spreading his benevolent smile around the workroom.

"Good morning, Mrs. Ehrlich." What seem like hundreds of large, white teeth are directed at me. "I hope you have found everything to your liking."

"Thank you, Mr. Levy. Everything is fine."

"Can you come to my office," he looks at his watch, "in, say, half an hour?"

His office is small and elegantly furnished. He pulls up a chair for me. His desk is covered with files and correspondence. Red velvet curtains are half-drawn.

"Please sit down. We have a lot to talk about. And we need to get to know each other, don't you think?" His teeth gleam.

On the walls are several framed awards from Germany. A large photograph of a slim lady stands on the desk. Her eyes are intelligent, her features delicate.

"My wife. You'll like her. We have a son—he's seventeen. He doesn't want to come into the business, though—he wants to study law. I suppose you are too young to have children?"

"I'm *not* too young," I say. "But I have no children."

"You need to learn the ropes as quickly as possible," he says. "We need to start on our spring collection, and you'll have to go to Paris." He looks for my reaction, catches my surprise, grins and shows his teeth. They are beginning to annoy me.

Alice brings coffee and smiles at me as she leaves the room.

"You don't take sugar? Are you slimming? Miss Stradler hardly ate at all. She missed her fiancé very much. He kept on telling her that there was going to be a war, and that she would get stuck here. She's too good for him. Miss Stradler is a very capable woman, a perfectionist. Lucky man! He will sleep in a well-made bed."

At six o'clock, I hurry to catch my bus. It crawls along Oxford Street, Edgware Road, Kilburn High Road. At Victoria Road, I jump off and race home, taking the stairs up to our room two at a time. Walter is chopping up onions for a stew.

"I'm going to Paris! He's sending me to Paris on my own! I'm going to see my friends again, the fashion shows, walk along the Champs-Elysées—hurrah!"

That night, I suddenly think about leaving Walter behind. He will be alone, and I will be without him. He must be thinking the same thing. We hold each other tightly.

In the morning, Walter asks, "How will you be able to go to Paris? You don't have a passport—we're stateless. Austria doesn't exist anymore."

I don't know what I'm going to do. I need a stateless paper, but I have no idea how to get one or how long it will take. I don't even know if Mr. Levy will be able to help—he has a German passport and hasn't encountered this problem before. But I underestimate him. Two days after I show him my Austrian passport and explain the situation, he hands me a British stateless document, which secures my reentry into England. Suddenly, he seems quite intelligent and charming.

10

March 1939, Paris

Dear Mother,

   *I saw a Frenchwoman with sapphire blue eyes like yours.
She wasn't as pretty as you, though. Isn't life full of surprises?
Here I am, in Paris, and it isn't so long ago that I thought
I had said good-bye to it forever. I am so happy to see it
again, even under a cloudy sky. Sometimes a weak sun breaks
through and brings back memories of our lovely autumns in
Vienna, when I waded through golden leaves. Do you remember? When I came home, you were waiting with hot chocolate
and whipped cream.*

   *Paris is full of foreigners. Cars and taxis still speed down
the wide, tree-lined boulevards. The food is still too rich, too
many sauces.*

   *On the surface, life here seems to be the same. Luxurious,
lighthearted. But deep down, I know they are afraid. I miss
you more than ever.*

   Trudi

12 April 1939

Dear Trudi,

The British Consulate has informed us that our visas are on the way to Vienna. They will tell us when we can collect them. Truderl, my child, I am praying. I am confused. There is so much to do, I don't know where to start. I wish you were here. No, I don't!

Your father sends his love.
Mother

104 George Street, W1, is in the middle of a row of tall, narrow, terraced houses. Mrs. Brindle, an old lady, opens the door.

"You've come to see the flat?"

She takes us up a narrow staircase to the first floor and opens the door to a large living room, the same size as our room in Victoria Road. Sunshine streams through the windows, spills out of the doorway, lingers on the landing. In my imagination, I have already moved in. Next to the living room, a well-equipped kitchen has white walls, a dark red tiled floor, plenty of light from a large window.

On the floor above are two good-size bedrooms and a white tiled bathroom.

"I'll leave you alone," Mrs. Brindle says. "You'll want to talk it over. Have a good look around. The rent is ten pounds a month, payment in advance."

"Walter, I love it!"

Walter hesitates. "I like it very much, but it's too expensive. We'll definitely be able to find something cheaper."

"I want this one," I sulk. "It's so central. I could walk to work; that would save money. We're so lucky to find a flat like this. Look, darling, I earn five pounds a week now, and you'll soon earn money yourself. We'll manage."

"Your parents will be here soon. There will be four of us. Money will be tight."

Three weeks later, we move in. Our large wooden crate from the storage facility in Holland arrives. We laugh when we unpack the rugs we stole from Walter's flat in Vienna. Here is my clock. Its chime has a soothing effect.

It is May; my parents are arriving tomorrow. I jump for joy, waving their telegram at Walter. I make vegetable soup, Father's favorite, and veal in lemon sauce, Mother's speciality. I bake a cake made with grated walnuts, sugar, chocolate. No flour.

Victoria Station, platform 11. The Golden Arrow is twenty minutes late.

"Let's find somewhere to sit down." Walter takes my arm.

"No! Please! I don't want to miss them."

Half an hour later, we hear the train approaching, a long hoot. There are sheets of white steam. Finally we see its broad black face, hear the screeching brakes. Doors open, people spill out, lots of people. I don't see my parents. I run alongside the train, all the way to the end. The crowds are thinning out as I run back.

"They're *not here*! What's happened?"

Walter gets on the train to look for them. Suddenly, through my tears, I see a tall, white-haired gentleman helping a tiny lady down the steps from the coach to the platform. My thin father. My shrunken mother.

I'll feed you. I'll love you. I'll make you forget.

PART EIGHT

The Phony War

(London, 1939)

1

On Sunday, 3 September 1939, I see a policeman wearing a tin hat. On top of our red pillar-box is a yellow square of gas-detector paint. The street is deserted. Everyone is listening, waiting, at home, abroad, at sea. Germany has invaded Poland; Warsaw is being bombed. The clock strikes eleven.

"The ultimatum has expired," Walter whispers.

I close the window. We sit at the kitchen table, staring at the wireless, trying to understand what Chamberlain is saying.

"Everything that I have worked for, everything that I had hoped for, everything that I had believed in during my public life, has crashed in ruins."

Outside, silver barrage balloons float in the blue sky.

"Now may God bless you all and may he defend the right, for it is evil things that we shall be fighting against, brute force, bad faith, injustice, oppression, and persecution. Against them I am certain that right will prevail. We are now at war with Germany."

As his thin voice fades away, the first air-raid warning

sounds loud and clear. A false alarm? A siren to shock us into the reality of war?

We rush to our "shelter," a coal cellar in front of our house. Nothing happens, so we go back inside.

War: gas masks, ration cards, trains full of soldiers.

We sit by the wireless and listen. All men between the ages of 17 and 65 were eligible for the Local Defence Volunteers; Air Raid Precautions were being organized, and the mass evacuation of children from cities to the countryside.

The shadow of war spread across Europe. No one believed Hitler's assurances that he was not interested in further conquests.

"This madman will not stop now." Father shakes his head. "France will be next, then us."

2

In July, about five weeks before the war began, Gina, Pepi's girlfriend, had telephoned. Her voice is shaky.

"Trudi, I'm so worried." Now she is crying. "Pepi arrives tomorrow at three o'clock."

"But that's good news, isn't it?"

"I'm so afraid that they won't let him in—I don't know what to do."

Next day, I wait at Croydon Airport for my ex-husband to arrive. I think about our wedding, the synagogue dressed in yellow and white flowers, garlands around the arches, hanging from the rails. There was a faint yellow scent in the air.

Why did I divorce him? Now that I am married to Walter, I have come to realize that there can't be red roses every day. A good marriage means having someone to talk to at night, someone you can fight with and fuss over. Someone you trust.

What will I do if they won't let Pepi in? If they discover the discrepancy between the date of birth on his passport and the one on his application form? They can't send him back to Hitler, can they? Surely they can't. I will fight for him. I'll smile at them; I'll cry. I realize I am twisting my handkerchief so hard I have nearly torn it.

And then I see him. Gray flannel trousers, white shirt, sleeves rolled up. He carries his hat in his hand. His thick, brown hair is disheveled. When he smiles, his full mouth splits wide open.

We run toward each other. I want to hold him for a long time.

Gina is waiting outside. I watch them embrace.

"It was all straightforward," I tell Walter later. "The immigration asked the usual questions and stamped Pepi's passport with an entry visa."

"How lucky."

"I'm not so sure it was luck. An English immigration

officer doesn't overlook a thing like that. I think he was a very kind man."

"You're right—but it's still lucky. How is Pepi?"

"The collar of his shirt is too big. There are lines under his eyes. I couldn't really talk to him—Gina was there. He's coming to see us on Sunday."

He comes regularly on Sundays. Once, he asks me, "Shall I marry Gina?"

"Do you love her?"

"Yes," he says, looking past me.

"Then you should marry her, of course. Why ask me?"

"I don't know," he says. He got married a few weeks later.

I have the flu. Pepi sits by my bed, drops the spoon, bends down to pick it up, and spills his coffee."

"Why are you so jumpy? Is something wrong?"

"Gina's pregnant."

"I envy her," I say unhappily.

"If you envy her, why don't you have a child?"

"We have tried, Pepi. The doctors can't find anything wrong, but still I don't get pregnant."

"It'll come, you'll see," he says, stroking my hand. "But Trudi, should we have the baby? I don't earn enough money to look after a family."

"It'll come, you'll see." I laugh. "Of course you must have the baby! You know that where there are children, God will provide?"

God did. Pepi found a very good job at a gentlemen's out-fitters in Great Portland Street. After his baby son was born, he brought him around every Sunday. Dicki was an exceptionally beautiful child. I loved playing with him; he would laugh and shriek and put his little arms around my neck.

Pepi missed his family who were now in America, and a few months later he, Gina, and Dicki left for New York.

The Home Office set up tribunals across Britain, run by lawyers, justices of the peace, and judges. They placed enemy aliens into one of three categories. Category A meant internment; Category B meant no internment but certain restrictions; Category C meant freedom. At the end of October, we were summoned to the town hall. As refugees from Nazi oppression, we were put in Category C—it all seemed very straightforward.

The term *phony war* was coined by American journalists. The war had not begun, and life seemed to be carrying on much as normal. True, all "places of entertainment" had been closed: there were no football matches, no swimming pools, cinemas, or theaters, no racing. And travel, food, clothes, and other necessities of life were subject to restrictions. But even so, it did not feel as though there was a war.

This sense of calm finally ended in April 1940, when the Maginot Line turned out to be the biggest fiasco in the history of warfare. France was defenseless, and on Saturday 14 June, the German army marched into a stunned Paris.

"You're crying!" Walter exclaimed, taking my hand.

My beautiful Paris. "What will happen to all my friends?"

"I know. I feel the same about my family in Prague. They haven't answered my last two letters."

A tiny pink and white dress . . .

Day by day, the news grew worse. Our visas from America finally arrived. But it was too late. No passenger liners were operating. We were trapped again, on an island, with the German army a few miles across the Channel.

PART NINE

A Letter

(London, 1940–45)

1

One morning, I overhear Gwen talking to Alice.

"It was unbelievable," she says. "Two plainclothes police-men! They had an internment order and took our German neighbors off to the police station. They—" She stops abruptly when she sees me enter the room. I pretend I haven't heard.

I sit at my desk and try to concentrate on some instruc-tions and notes from our factory in Luton, but I can't take in a single word. Gwen and Alice are busy at their desks; Gwen's face is flushed, and she keeps glancing at me.

It was only a few weeks ago that we were officially classed as "friendly aliens." So why am I so worried?

When I go home for lunch, I notice two men sitting in a maroon car parked opposite our house. Are they plainclothes policemen? I rush upstairs and watch the car through the net curtains of our sitting room windows. Mother is mak-ing lunch; pots and pans rattle in the kitchen. She is singing. The car moves farther up the street, then reverses. The driver seems to be looking at our front door.

The car is still there when I leave to go back to work. I don't say anything to Mother. But all afternoon I feel sick. Mr. Levy is out, and I leave early.

As I pass our landlady's door, she opens it. Her cheeks are very pink. She is very fond of Walter, who sometimes does her shopping for her.

"Mrs. Ehrlich," she whispers. "Don't be upset. I'm sure it's nothing, maybe just routine. It must be. You and Mr. Ehrlich! No. No!"

I grip the banister. "What is it, Mrs. Brindle? What are you trying to tell me?"

"The police were here. This afternoon. Two of them, asking for your husband and your father. I said they were out. It's nothing, isn't it?"

"I'm sure it's nothing," I lie.

Mother is at home. "Trudi, I've made minced meat today, and carrots with a little sugar and parsley—Walter loves it like that."

The four of us sit down to dinner. Mother watches us enjoying our food. "It's lovely, Mother. Thank you," I say. How am I going to tell them?

I wait for Walter to finish, then break the bad news.

Into the silence that follows, Walter says, "Tomorrow, they'll come to intern us. Father, we must pack a few things."

Mother's face is shocked. "Why? What have you done?" She puts her cup down. Her hand is shaking, and she spills coffee on the white tablecloth.

"Nothing. They are going to intern us because England is

at war with our country, and since the fall of France and the news of fifth columnists, they are terrified of spies, and terrified of an invasion. This is only a small island. If the Germans really have spies here, then all is lost."

Father says, "But all the refugees are on England's side! We want England to win!"

"*We* know that, but *they* don't," Walter says. "And they won't take us to a concentration camp. We're going to be interned, that's all."

"God knows what can happen, once you're behind locked doors."

"It won't be long, you'll see." Walter pats Mother's hand. He strokes my cheek, lifts my chin, looks into my anxious eyes. "It'll be all right, darling."

"Where are our suitcases?" Father's voice is choked. He is trying to hide his feelings, but I know that he's desperate.

"In the loft," I say. "Walter will fetch them."

Walter gets up and leaves the table. Mother shakes her head. Father's slim fingers move bread crumbs around on the tablecloth.

A few minutes later, we hear a loud crash from the bathroom. I run in there. The bath, basin, and floor are covered in rubble. Walter's legs are hanging through the ceiling.

"Walter! Walter!" I scream. "Are you all right?" I hear him laughing.

Walter is determined to repair the damage there and then. "We can't afford to pay a builder," he says. "If Mrs. Brindle finds out, there'll be trouble. I'll lock all the doors and close the windows. We won't let anyone into this place to take me away before I've finished the job!"

He spends half the night replastering the ceiling, covering it with a temporary arrangement of newspaper and paint.

I pack his suitcase. White short-sleeved shirts with a breast pocket where he puts his cigarettes. Oxford shirts, strong, heavy material. He loves his gray tweed jacket with four pockets. A gray cardigan to match his flannel trousers. Will they let him wear it? Good God—surely they won't put them in prison uniforms? I am suddenly back at 11 Kohlmarkt, packing his things so they won't be found at my flat, terrified. My hands are shaking so much I can't fold his shirts.

Normally, people pack when they go on holiday.

Walter comes into the bedroom, exhausted. His hands are red and raw where he has had to scrub off the paint. It's three a.m. I cling to him. He kisses me gently.

"You must be brave. You have to take care of your mother, and of our home. Nothing and no one can come between us. Don't ever forget that."

"I can't live without you," I say. There are white flecks of paint in his damp, black hair.

"It won't be long. You'll see."

"How long? This is unbearable. In Vienna, I could try to protect you. Here, I am helpless. What can I do?"

"Be hopeful. Keep on loving me. Write to me, often."

"How? Where will they take you? What are they going to do to you?"

I cry and cry. I can't stop. It is a dark, painful night.

The doorbell rings at six thirty a.m. Walter looks out of the window.

"A black van," he says. He slips into his trousers. Shirtless, he runs to the landing to go downstairs and open the front door. I stop him.

"You can't! You mustn't!" I shout. "They'll grab you right off the doorstep! Take my parents into the sitting room, quickly!"

Mother stumbles into our room, fiddling with her hairpins. I help her into her blue dressing gown. Father, in his striped pajamas, follows.

"Nesti, Nesti, careful," he says. He carries his slippers. He is rubbing his forefinger against his thumb, as he does when he is agitated. His white hair is ruffled.

I dress quickly. The bell rings again, insistently.

"The henchmen are here," Father says bitterly.

I go downstairs myself and open the door to two men in dark civilian clothes. "Police," they say, and show me a card. They follow me upstairs into the sitting room.

Walter has got dressed; he is wearing his red pullover. Father stands with his arm around Mother's shoulders. There they are, a thin, frail old couple. They have survived a pogrom; they spent eight frightening months in Nazi Vienna, waiting

for their visas, waiting to be allowed to come to England—
for refuge.

"We have a warrant," the senior officer explains. He produces a letter authorizing them to take "one Walter Ehrlich"
and "one Adolf Sturmwind" into custody.

"Are you Walter Ehrlich?" He points at Walter.

"I am," Walter replies.

"And you are Adolf Sturmwind?" he asks my father.

"*Jawohl*," Father says.

"What?"

"He doesn't speak English," Walter explains. "It means
yes."

The policeman tells Father to get dressed.

"Where are you taking them?" I ask.

"To Albany Street police station."

"And then?"

"We don't know, madame." The officer looks at the ceiling;
the other one looks at his boots.

"For how long?"

"We don't know, madame." His voice is cool.

"Why are you taking them? What have they done?"

"They're Austrians," the senior officer says. "We have our
instructions. Sorry."

Mother starts to cry. I am fighting back tears myself. *You
can't do this. He's mine.*

We embrace, one hug that has to last for a long time. How
long? What is long? One day without Walter seems an eternity.

Walter picks up the suitcases. I will never forget the hurt look in his eyes, the desperate expression, the wordless good-bye.

The front door closes behind them. I stand in the sitting room, quite still. Memories race through my mind. The deer dance up the hill in the Vienna woods. Walter sits far away—too far away—from me on my sofa. His eyes are purple as he kisses me in the dark. Mother likes him. We sit huddled together on the glass roof.

2

COLLAR THE LOT the headlines demand. Until one newspaper publishes an article describing the misery that internment has caused innocent people. Suddenly, the tide turns: FREE USEFUL ALIENS the headlines shout. FREE INNOCENT INTERNEES.

In London, I look after Mother, try to stop her crying, go to work, wait for the postman. She sleeps next to me in our bed. I have to hide in the cloakroom to cry.

The Levys don't mind when I arrive late for work, or leave early. They try to help. Fritz tells me that when the German army marched into the south of France, some commanders of the internment camps there opened the gates and told the refugees to run.

But others locked them in.

Where is Walter? I sit in the large, cold workroom at the Clarendon Hat Company, missing my cozy, shimmering workroom at Kohlmarkt, where we designed our hats for their beauty, rather than for a certain price range.

A letter arrives with the address handwritten in the English style, the street number before the street name. I open it with shaking hands. Inside is a torn-off flap of another envelope. Written on it in pencil are the words, "*Wir sind gesund*" ("We are all right"). It's Father's handwriting. I try to imagine how he got this message to an English person who in turn got it to me. And what does the message mean? Is Walter ill? How did Father communicate with an English person? Did he use sign language? Maybe he wrote down our address, pointed to it, pointed to my name, and said, "daughter"? I can see it all—the Englishman would have asked if he wanted to write a message, gave him an old envelope. He was a kind Englishman; he addressed another envelope and posted the message. Where could they have met? Maybe it was a kind guard on the train? Father is charming, tall, patrician-looking. Men like that. That must be how it happened. Mother and I agree.

That evening, after Mother has gone to bed, I'm reading the newspaper:

Yesterday, 2 July 1940, the 15,000-ton liner *Arandora Star* was torpedoed and sunk in the Atlantic, west of Ireland. The luxury liner had sailed from Liverpool on 1 July. Bound for Canada, she carried British men, Italians, and Germans. The Germans comprised the strangest mixture, from Nazis to Jews, businessmen to revolutionaries and socialists. Some were fanatical supporters of the Third Reich, others were refugees from Nazi persecution who had left friends and relatives in German concentration camps. Some did not consider themselves German at all, but Austrian, and had fled their country after Hitler annexed it in 1938. Each of these groups were represented among the *Arandora Star*'s survivors on that mild, midsummer morning in July 1940. Each was represented, unevenly, among those who died.

My blood runs cold. I rush into the kitchen and snatch Father's message up off the table.

It was posted in Liverpool on 29 June.

I sit down. I mustn't wake Mother.

Hours later, the first rays of light break through the window. They lie in thin stripes on the red kitchen floor. I hear the first bird sing.

A small, copper-framed art nouveau mirror belonging to my mother hangs on the kitchen wall. When she heard the front door close and recognized my father's tread, she would stand in front of it, rearranging her hairpins, pinching her cheeks to give them color, straightening her apron. When he came into the kitchen, he would find a pretty, smiling wife, awaiting his kiss. This mirror now reflects my white, worried face.

How can I find out where Walter and Father are?

* * *

For the next two days, I live in hourly fear of a telegram. I sit uneasily in the kitchen, listening to the hiss of the boiling coffee machine. The milkman rattles bottles and churns on the pavement. Finally, the postman brings the mail.

I run downstairs. There is a letter addressed to me from His Majesty's Government, Internment Camp, Huyton, near Liverpool. It is from Walter and is written on shiny prison paper—I find out later on that it is designed to repel invisible ink. Internees are allowed to write eighteen lines. Walter writes that he and Father are both well and that they are together, and he asks us to send warm clothes.

Alive. Not at the bottom of the sea. Now that I know they are safe, even though they are interned, I can breathe again. I hug my mother, and we dance together around the kitchen.

Why do they want warm clothes—do they expect to be there through the winter? My mother is annoyed that I didn't tell her about the *Arandora Star*. She asks again and again if I am absolutely certain that Father is with Walter.

We send sweets, tinned food, and winter clothes.

But my relief doesn't last long. After hearing about an internee being shot by mistake in an internment camp, I decide that I must visit Walter and see for myself how things are. I find a solicitor, Felix Hartley, an Anglo-German who is an expert on internee problems. He tells me that the War Office does not allow family of internees to visit; the only visitors allowed are lawyers. Luckily, he has a friend, Mr.

Cohen, who is going to Huyton to see another internee, and he will ask about Walter.

"When will he be able to give me some news?"

"You can ring him at his office first thing Monday morning."

It is Friday; the weekend drags by. On Monday morning, I ring Mr. Cohen.

"Mr. Cohen? This is Mrs. Ehrlich. I believe you visited my husband in Huyton?"

"Yes, that is correct."

"How is he?"

"Mrs. Ehrlich, I'm afraid I have to tell you that your husband has been deported to Australia. He is on the *Dunera*, which sailed from Liverpool for Sydney carrying two thousand two hundred and fifty deportees."

I might never see Walter again.

"Hello, are you still there?" Mr. Cohen asks.

"Are you certain?" My voice cracks.

"I'm afraid so. I spoke to the camp commander."

"And my father?"

"I had no instructions pertaining to your father, so I'm afraid I don't know."

"Can you tell me anything else?"

"It would be best for you to speak to Mr. Hartley."

Why did I dance Mother around the kitchen?

"Walter would never leave your father alone," Mother says, trying to reassure me. I agree. Surely they are together.

There is nobody to whom I can appeal, nobody who

will understand, nobody I can even allow to see my misery. Nobody is on my side.

I send a telegram to the Balfours, who helped us with my father's visa:

OUR HUSBANDS HAVE BEEN DEPORTED TO
AUSTRALIA STOP PLEASE CAN YOU HELP US
TO BE INTERNED WITH THEM STOP

We go to see them at their house in London and explain what has happened. Lord Balfour makes inquiries of a friend of his at the Home Office, but nothing comes of it; it is not possible for us to be interned with Father and Walter. He himself is shocked about the deportations. "What has happened to my country?" he asks, shaking his head.

I still cannot believe that I might never see Walter again.

I send a telegram to the camp commander at Huyton:

WHERE IS MY HUSBAND WALTER EHRLICH STOP

And I get a telegram in reply:

WE ARE WELL STOP LETTER FOLLOWS STOP WALTER

The telegram was sent by permission of the camp commander himself.

Another Walter Ehrlich is on his way to Australia.

It is August. The heat is unbearable, but at least I know that Walter and Father are well. Long days of blazing sunshine have melted the tar on Baker Street. I look up into a still, blue sky filled with fat, silver barrage balloons.

I have to find a way to visit the camp.

He sat at an old desk, crammed with correspondence, order sheets, bolts, screws, clamps. Pens and pencils were strewn across it. A bottle of whiskey, a flask of water, and two glasses were on a tray balanced on the corner of the desk.

Mr. Curlow, the owner of a manufacturing company called Mica Products, was a massive man with a sharp eye for business. He had agreed in principle to mass-produce one of Walter's inventions: a bright red cigarette box that you could carry in your pocket but that opened up like folding steps that you could stand on the table for people to help themselves.

The financial agreement between Walter and Mr. Curlow was nearly complete when Walter was interned. This is why I have come to see him. I admire the factory through the office window, the delivery vans coming and going. Mr. Curlow is a man who has worked his way up from the bottom. He came to London from Cornwall as a boy: "I said good-bye to my parents and never looked back."

"You didn't have to. You're a great success."

Our eyes met.

"What can I do for you, young lady?"

"My husband can't contact you. He's not allowed to write more than one letter every two weeks. So he has asked me to finalize the deal."

"That's not so easy." Mr. Curlow shook his head. "He has to guarantee to give his technical advice for the production of his patent whenever we need it."

"I can help you with that. Usually only lawyers are allowed to visit internment camps. But if you give me a letter stating that you need technical advice which only Walter can give, they might let me see him."

His green eyes were probing. He called in his secretary and dictated the letter.

"Get in touch when you get back," he said. "Good luck, my dear."

3

The train to Liverpool was packed. People stood in the corridors. A dark-eyed girl looked through the glass door at me. Her eyes sparkled. I opened the door and offered her my seat for a while. She hesitated, and an elderly man spoke up: "I'm sure we can make room for the young lady."

Now five people were sitting on a bench for four. Luckily, the girl was very slim. Sitting next to me, she told me that her name was Mimi and she was going to Huyton to visit her interned husband. She was Viennese and had a great sense of humor.

"How do you keep so slim?"

"It all goes here," she said, patting her full behind. "And thank God—that's what he loves me for."

Once we reached Liverpool, we shared a taxi from the station.

Some of them stand close to the long barbed-wire fence, peering out to see who is coming; others walk around with hunched shoulders, their heads down, not expecting anyone. A cold wind is blowing. It wouldn't be quite so bad if they were in uniform, but they wear old suit jackets, overcoats, and scarves; some are freezing in shirtsleeves. I can't see Walter or Father. I run up and down the fence, searching. Where are they?

A soldier escorts us to an office. I sign a document stating that I am entering the camp at my own risk. German airplanes come and go overhead.

I rush outside. Why can't I see them? Walter knows I'm coming. What's happened? I think of the man who was shot by accident in an internment camp. I'm frantic. And then, upon a hill, I see a man with white hair that is blowing in the wind.

"Father!" I'm shaking.

He strokes my hair. His eyes are dull.

"Where's Walter?" I ask. "Is he all right?"

"He's right next to you," Father says.

I turn. Walter's olive skin has turned white. There are blue shadows under his eyes. He takes my hand and leads me across rough, hilly ground into a large, long room. A bare wooden table runs the length of it. At each end of the table stands a soldier, bayonet up. On each side of it are narrow wooden benches. The internees have to sit on one side, visitors on the other.

Walter. My father. Prisoners. I want to cry. I hold Walter's hand under the table. Our every move is watched by the soldiers.

"Mother sends her love," I say.

"How are you managing?" Father asks.

"We miss you."

"How's Mother taking it? I'm so worried about her. We've never been parted before."

"She sleeps in the bed with me. She doesn't cry. She's being very brave."

Walter's face is so strained. "Are you ill?" I ask. "Why are you so pale?"

"There's nothing to worry about. I've got an inflamed bladder, that's all."

"Is it painful?"

"Much better now." He smiles.

"How did you get it?"

"When they brought us here, Huyton was an unfinished council-housing estate. You can't imagine what it was like. Piles of rubble everywhere. There weren't enough houses, so they pitched tents in a nearby field. I managed to get Father into a house with eleven other internees. It wasn't finished, but at least he had a roof over his head, and it was dry. I had to go into a tent. They gave us a sack each and told us to stuff it with straw to make a palliasse."

"What's a palliasse?" I ask.

"A kind of mattress," Father explains. "Very uncomfortable. Anyway, it took Walter a while to get into a house. We had no towels, no lavatory paper, a one-ounce tablet of soap per week."

I put my hand in front of my mouth. I feel so sorry for them.

"It promptly rained, of course," Walter says. "The field became a sea of mud. It's not surprising I've had bladder trouble."

"How can this happen in England?" I shake my head.

"It all happened too quickly. They didn't know what they were doing—they were panic-stricken," says Walter.

"You always defend them!" My father is bitter. "Tell her how they banned newspapers, books, the wireless. They censored our letters, and we had to wait ages before we got them. It made us feel so isolated. Why do they punish us like this? We're on their side."

Walter winks at me. "I have something top secret to tell you," he whispers. "I was offered release from internment if I agreed to join the Pioneer Corps, a voluntary labor force for foreigners. I would have been sent overseas to dig trenches and do other work—not fighting, because they wouldn't issue us with weapons. They said they would give us English names on our papers, in case we got taken prisoner. Then last week I was taken to see the officer in charge of the camp. He told me to sit down, gave me a cigarette, and said, 'Ehrlich, I don't want you to join the Pioneer Corps, not while you are an internee. This is a decision one should make as a free man. Is that clear?' 'Yes, sir,' I said. 'Thank you.'"

"He knew you would have been in double danger—if you had been captured, they would have known immediately that you are both Austrian and Jewish. And you wouldn't even have a weapon."

"The commander has taken a liking to Walter," Father says. "He's given him some work in his office."

"It makes life much easier," Walter says. "And I'm trying to help some of the internees."

"Well, I'm glad you're no longer just a number," I say. "How's the food?"

"It's not like Nesti's goulash." Father chuckles. "Boiled cabbage, cold sausages, meat pies—ugh."

"Do you get enough to eat?"

"Who wants more of that?"

"Can you buy extra?"

"They took all our money when we got here. We can draw five shillings a week to spend in the canteen and for cigarettes."

Father sees me smuggling an envelope into Walter's hand underneath the table. I have scraped together twenty pounds for them.

Other visitors have come in since we started talking. Wives, sons, daughters, fiancées, friends.

I tell Walter about Mr. Curlow and Mica Products and ask him what I should do.

He shrugs. "I leave it all up to you, darling. Whatever you say."

One of the soldiers glances at his watch. How much time do we have?

Father's hands are rough and chapped. "Don't tell Nesti of our troubles," he says. "Give her my love and tell her how much I miss her."

Walter's hair needs cutting.

A bell rings. The parting is brief. Walter's badly shaved face rubs against my cheek. "There are rumors of a German invasion," I whisper.

"I know, darling. We've found a hole in the perimeter fence. It won't be difficult to enlarge it." Then, more loudly, he says, "Keep well, darling. Love to Mother." He squeezes my hands. Father's eyes fill with tears.

I am on the other side of the barbed-wire fence, dazed. It is nearly dark. Someone touches my shoulder; it is Mimi, crying.

We reach Liverpool in the middle of a terrible air raid. It is 7 September 1940. Planes roar over us. We hear the whistle of falling bombs. Explosions. Dust and gravel fly through the air. We run to the nearest hotel.

The staff and guests are crowded into a basement ball-room, along with people like us who have come in off the street. A baby crawls along by the wall. A little girl's face has been blackened. She bawls. We are lucky to find a corner.

Mimi and I sit on the parquet floor, huddled together, too tired to talk.

It is impossible to leave Liverpool that night. Bombs rain down. I can't sleep. The visit to the camp has upset me badly. And I'm worried about Mother, who is expecting me at home. What if there is a big air raid in London? She's always afraid to be left alone.

Finally, the painful night ends. I hear the all clear and rush to the telephone. Mother cries when she hears my voice.

"It's all right, Mother. They're well. They send their love. I'll tell you all the news as soon as I'm back, but I don't know when I'll be home—trains are very slow. But please don't worry."

We are told to report to the police station—foreigners are permitted to travel through Liverpool but not to stay. The police want to see our documents. They question us. We plead and beg and explain. It takes an hour to persuade them to let us go. There are no buses, so we have to walk. The streets are littered with rubble and glass. Water pipes have burst, and jets of water shoot up everywhere. All the shops are closed, but luckily the station café is open. We have breakfast and buy some stale sandwiches for the journey.

The train seems to stop at every single station. Our compartment is full. Mimi manages to get two cups of weak tea. She is upset about her husband.

"He's so unhappy. Sharing good times is one thing, sharing bad times is another. I wake up in a comfortable bed, and I feel so guilty. I eat good food and remember what he gets, how little his five shillings will buy him. I'm not even talking about freedom—do you understand?"

"Yes. Thank God Walter and my father have each other, and I did manage to give Walter some money under the table."

Mimi is upset she didn't think of giving her husband money.

Suddenly, the lights go out. We are coming into London in the middle of another air raid. There are strict blackout regulations. Even the tiny light of a cigarette could be dangerous.

We are on a ghost train, talking in low voices. The other passengers are whispering shadows. As we approach the suburbs, I hear a man's shocked voice: "Good God, they must have bombed the docks! Look at the sky!"

It is in flames. It looks like an abstract painting: red, pink, purple. Heavy smoke merges with clouds; gashes of red gleam through them. Swishing sounds of falling bombs. Slowly, slowly, the driver shunts the train into a tunnel. I grip Mimi's hand. I don't know how long we wait there. Then brakes screech, and we're off again.

The train draws into St. Pancras. Bewildered passengers mill about on the platform, wondering how to get home; there are no trains, buses, or taxis. The blackout is still in force, but the sky is lit by the burning docks. Shadowy figures move about, asking each other questions, trying to find a way home.

I turn to ask Mimi where she lives, but I can't see her. I

walk on, glancing back; she has vanished. Suddenly I have a painful feeling of loneliness. The day, the night, the shared journey, and now Mimi's disappearance: a ghost story. I sit on a bench to wait for daylight to come.

I hear someone call my name. It is Felix Hartley, my solicitor. He was on the same train as I; he, too, has been visiting internees. He has his car and is going my way.

4

Mr. Curlow wants to show me the City of London during an air raid. It is a damp September night. Mist rises from the Thames, lingering in the narrow streets. Bombs are falling in the distance; fires blaze everywhere.

"Are you afraid?" His strong gaze seeks mine.

"Not at all," I say. I am too shy to meet his eyes.

"You're cold!" He puts an arm around my shoulder as if to protect me from the mist, the fires, the bombs. He stops his car in the middle of the deserted London Bridge. We get out and look down the river. He is tall and powerful. In this unreal light, his dark hair looks blond. Even in my new white raincoat, I feel small and unimportant next to him. Searchlights outline the edges of the clouds. Luminous rays sweep across the dark sky.

I have left Mother in the shelter. Mr. Curlow takes me back there. We stand at the church entrance.

"Thank you for everything," I say.

"It was my pleasure." The thunder of antiaircraft guns drowns his voice. "We didn't talk much about business." White teeth glint in the darkness. "I want to get the agreement finalized. Will you ring me tomorrow?"

"Yes." He doesn't know yet, but I need another favor from him.

"Tomorrow, then." He kisses my cheek. The nearness of him makes my skin sensitive.

I am frantic because I haven't heard from Walter. When I telephone Mr. Curlow the next day, I beg him to help me. "I need a letter. Please help me—I'm desperate . . ."

"Calm down," he says. "Let me take you out to dinner tonight. It will be easier to discuss things. I'll pick you up outside the shelter at eight."

In a Chinese restaurant in Soho, we sit at a corner table. Bright red linen tablecloth and napkins, tall white candles in wrought-iron candlesticks, white walls painted with scrolls. Mr. Curlow hands me the menu. I don't know anything about Chinese food. There were no Chinese restaurants in Vienna. I ask him to order for me.

The waiter wears a white shirt with huge sleeves, black trousers. A large red napkin is tucked into his leather belt as an apron.

"Well?" Curlow's eyes behind his glasses seem turbulent. He is aging, but his lips are full, his chin square. He is tough without being coarse. His vehemence and his brilliance attract me.

"You asked me to help you. Now, my dear, tell me all about it."

I explain. The newspapers have been campaigning for useful aliens to be released from internment. I have to prove that Walter is such a person. I must get him out of that terrible place. I need Mr. Curlow to write a letter for the Home Office, saying that he needs Walter for essential war work in his factory and giving a guarantee of employment.

Curlow studies his manicured fingernails.

"You know Walter has talent," I say.

The food arrives. Five warming plates with two dishes on each are placed on the table. Curlow explains what each exotic dish is, and puts a portion from each on my plate. Prawns are fried golden in batter. I love the sweet-and-sour pork, the duck sliced into narrow strips and roasted with caraway seeds, the fried rice, the crispy noodles. What a change from our usual wartime fare.

"Help yourself to the vegetables. The Chinese fry them lightly so they don't lose their flavor. The bean sprouts are delicious." He hands me a bottle. "Soy sauce: the Chinese salt."

We eat in silence. Then Mr. Curlow says, "Mrs. Ehrlich. Trudi. Did you come here tonight because you wanted to have dinner with me? Or did you come because you need me to write the letter?"

"That's a difficult question," I say.

"Don't stall, my dear. Yes or no?"

"I don't know."

"Don't be childish. An experienced young woman like you knows her own feelings."

"Don't make me say something I might come to regret. I didn't come here to row."

"I'm glad to help you out, of course. But I don't like being taken for a ride." His eyes are contemptuous now.

"How dare you! You insisted I come tonight. And now you are trying to force me into saying things I know I will regret. It's like blackmail."

"You've gone too far now!" He bangs the table. People are staring.

"I want to go home," I shout at him.

We go to the shelter in silence. Outside the entrance, he starts again. "Trudi. Was it me? Or was it the damned letter?"

"I have nothing to say."

Roofs and chimneys are silhouetted against the red sky. Mr. Curlow vanishes into the night. There is a sudden feeling of absence once he has gone. I want to cry. Is this my fault? Even in my smart clothes, with my sophisticated maquillage, my two marriages, and all my recent experiences, I am still an immature girl.

I go into the shelter. The all clear has sounded, and most people have already gone back home. Mother is sitting by herself on a bench, her hands folded in her lap.

On the way home, she says, "Why did you go out with that man? You're a married woman. It's not right!"

I explain about the letter I need for Walter.

In the double bed, next to Mother, I try to sleep, but I am too restless. I ache for Walter. And I can see Mr. Curlow's face. His features are thick and stubborn, like his body. He is powerful. *Walter, hold me, I can't see you.*

Early in the morning, I hear Mother downstairs. The blackout blinds are still drawn. Mr. Curlow's letter to the Home Office about Walter was posted through our letter box during the night. There is no message for me.

5

He stands in the doorway: white, wild hair, sparkling eyes. Mother runs to him.

"Trudi, Trudi, Father is home!" She stands on tiptoe, trying to put her arms around his neck. "Sit down, take that old coat off. I'll get you something to eat." She rushes into the kitchen, singing.

"Father, sit down and tell me about Walter."

"He's fine, darling. He hopes to be home soon. And since the Home Office took over the internment camps, things have improved. Now there's toilet paper, soap. The food is better. We don't feel as though we are the enemy anymore. Letters are still censored, of course. But don't worry about Walter. He's sharing a good house with nice people and enjoys his work in the office. Did you know that Walter is a born organizer?"

Mother is radiant. She and Father didn't stop talking. When the siren went, Father came down to the shelter with us for the first time.

I missed Walter.

And three days later, I was holding him in my arms. There are shadows under his eyes. Hand in hand, we climb the stairs to our room.

"I have some news," I say. "Fritz Levy came to the shelter the other night. And not to see how we were doing. Not to ask if Mother was all right. He came to give me notice. He told me that the girls were spending more time in the shelter than in the workroom. He was losing money. 'Paying for nothing,' he said, 'is the fastest way to lose a business.' He gave me a check for the exact amount he owed me and left. Then the next day, Otto Levy telephoned and asked me to go and work for him in Luton. The salary is the same. Expenses will be paid. I'll have to travel thirty miles each way, but it'll be worth it—I'll have a job."

"I need to find a job myself," Walter says. "I'll see Curlow tomorrow."

I decide not to say anything about my meetings with Curlow. I don't want to turn Walter against him. We still need his help.

* * *

Walter started working at Mica as a laborer, earning three pounds a week. He traveled every day to Dalston. Then one day, as I came in from work, I found Walter sitting on the sofa looking completely beaten.

"What is it?" I ask. Walter stares out of the window. "Tell me."

That morning, Walter had arrived at work to find the men staring in disbelief at the bombed-out, cracked walls and charred planks of their factory.

"There was nothing left," Walter said. "Just a black hole. The men sat down, smoked, and waited for the boss."

I knew that Mica Products was the secret center of Mr. Curlow's heart. My eyes filled with tears, but Walter didn't know the real reason; I was crying for Mr. Curlow. He had behaved like a gentleman. Even after our row, he had given me the letter that had freed Walter from internment, and then he had employed him. "Curlow had a plan." Walter was smiling now. "'We'll build it all up again, everything as it was,' he said. 'Brick by brick, floors and ceilings, water and electricity. All of it! Who is with me?' The men stood up one by one. Trudi, can you imagine, underneath the snowy sky, a thin voice started to sing, and everyone gradually joined in, louder and louder, 'For he's a jolly good fellow, for he's a jolly good fellow . . .'"

* * *

Every morning, for many months, Walter put on his skiing outfit and traveled to work. He laid bricks, plastered walls, relaid electrical wiring, repaired machines. On the first day, when he returned home, I opened the door and nearly closed it again: outside stood a chimney sweep, black from top to toe. I recognized the blue eyes, and I kissed the black man. Every night after that, I gave him a large glass of brandy and helped him to undress. In his incredibly dirty face, his eyes were shining.

6

The air-raid shelter we use is in the basement of a small church in Baker Street. It is run by people from the church, who provide tea and biscuits and prayers and keep the shelter clean.

One night, the bombing is the worst we have ever experienced. Even in the shelter, we hear the noise of exploding bombs, followed by the crash of falling masonry.

I sit on a bench next to my parents, listening to the roar of the planes. Hitler followed us to Prague and now to London. Maybe we are being bombed by Austrian airmen.

The shelter marshal announces that all able-bodied men are needed outside. Walter jumps up and runs upstairs. A few minutes later, I follow him. I stop at the entrance. The street is an inferno. I stare at the remains of Druce's furniture store. The warden tells me it had a direct hit. Yellow, red-edged flames hiss viciously. They stretch long tongues and tails, twisting them left and right, driven by a strong wind, devouring everything they touch.

A man in a blue tweed sports jacket comes out of the shelter. He leans against a wall, smokes, adjusts his red tie, smiles.

"Why are you smiling?" I ask angrily.

"I love to see a fire," he replies, captivated by the flames. "Look at it." His voice is drunk with excitement. "Listen to the furious noises. The flames are eating and eating, fighting each other. Watch it!"

I watch, fascinated and frightened. Flames eat through the roof. The whole sky is yellow and pink. It is nighttime, the blackout is in force, yet in Baker Street it is daylight. We are a perfect target for the stream of bombers overhead. Where is Walter? I can't go down to the shelter. I have to wait here. Walter's in danger. Again.

Druce's is a shell, lit by fire from inside. It reminds me of my dollhouse. We used to put candles in it to achieve this effect.

It is raining bombs. There is a tremendous explosion. My ears are ringing. I'm terrified. My hair is full of dust, it sticks in my eyes and covers my clothes. I sway and almost fall. The man holds and steadies me.

"Why don't you go downstairs, miss?"

"My husband is out here!"

I run up and down Baker Street. There are fires all around me. I can't see through the smoke. I turn into George Street, and there he is. He's with another man, running toward a smoldering heap of rubble that moments ago was a house.

The sky is streaked with reddish-gold specks. Large gray flakes, high up above the fire, dance, twirl, twist, and sail down slowly, vanishing as they touch the ground. The flames are greedy beasts, beautiful and wild. The crackling and hissing makes them vicious.

Ambulances and first-aid vans start to arrive. Doctors, soldiers, and civilians try to help. Cups of tea appear. A baby lies on the pavement, crying. I run to him. His mother is digging and digging in the rubble. To find the father? Blood and dirt on her hands, tears running down her grimy face. Her hair sticks to her cheeks. She won't let me pick up the baby. A young man climbs out of a window, hangs on to the sill as the wall of a neighboring house collapses. Buildings cave in, as if crushed by a giant foot. Clouds of dust and smoke burst into the air.

Walter is digging in the rubble, looking for people who are trapped. A tall young girl stands in the middle of the road, paralyzed. I grip her arm, try to move her, but it is as though she is riveted to the road. I try to persuade her to come with me, but she can't hear me, and her eyes don't see me. I stroke her dusty, blond hair. Tears fall down her frozen face. "Mother," she whispers. Has she seen her mother, trapped, pinned under wreckage, dead?

Eventually she moves, and I lead her along the burning

street to the church door. I ask the man in the blue jacket to take her down to the shelter.

I run back along George Street. Walter is still digging. In Baker Street, people lie buried under beams and floorboards. A hand sticks out of the rubble, the top of someone's head. I'm going to be sick. A boy lies pinned under part of a roof. He is in agony; he tries to smile. An old woman, grateful for a mug of tea, jokes about the missing sugar.

The bombers are coming back. I rush back to the church and go down into the shelter to see if my parents are all right. It is packed. Mother struggles through the crowd toward me. She is crying.

"I was so worried. Why have you been so long?" She flings her arms around me. "Where's Walter? What a terrible raid. Just look at all these people." Father, tears in his eyes, grips my hand.

Walter joins us, his face and clothes black with grime. His left hand is bandaged—he tried to pick up some metal rods that were too hot to handle. I stroke his hair.

"It was terrible, darling. Terrible," Walter says. He gropes for my hand. I am proud of him.

More and more people crowd into the shelter. Some have to sit on the flagstone floor. They are dressed in their nightclothes. There is a huge unexploded bomb in Portman Square. We don't know if our houses will still be there when we go outside. *If* we go outside. We are safe only from blast— not from a direct hit.

A huge man with ginger hair is standing in front of my father, poking a thick finger in his chest. "Bloody enemy aliens! You have no right to be in here—your planes are killing our people. Go home!"

Walter leaps at him. The man shakes him off easily and knees him in the stomach. Walter punches him in the face. Mother covers her eyes. Father has gone white.

The shelter marshal, a slim young priest, shouts, "Stop this at once! These people have every right to be here."

The man carries on shouting: "We need their places. Bloody traitors!"

"Look at him," says the priest, pointing at Walter with his bandaged hand. "He's bleeding. He's exhausted from trying to rescue people. You—what have *you* done to help?" He pushes the man into another room.

We sit huddled together on our benches. People gather around, making it clear they are on our side.

The all clear sounds at dawn. We can go home. People scramble for the exit. We are carrying our mattresses and have to pick our way through the rubble. Mother walks slowly. I take her arm. Walter carries her mattress. Fires are still smoldering everywhere. No water is left to douse them. But our building is still standing.

At home, exhausted, we climb the stairs to our bedrooms. There is a brown spot on the ceiling in my parents' room, and when Father touches it, it is warm. Walter opens the trapdoor to the loft, and flames leap out at him. He shuts it again, runs downstairs, and telephones the fire brigade, who arrives in minutes. Bells ringing, headlights full-on, the fire engine stops in front of our house. Firemen in high black boots climb ladders, drag long hoses through the window. They wrench open the trapdoor and douse the flames.

During the night, an incendiary had crashed through the roof and into the loft, which was full of old clothes and broken chairs, piles of magazines and papers. But the device landed on the small metal plate of one of Walter's skis.

The wood used for skis does not burn easily. For many hours, the bomb sat on the metal, gradually heating it. Eventually, the wood began to smolder, and when Walter opened the trapdoor, it was ignited by the draft.

7

"This is a war of the unknown warriors," Churchill told the world in the summer of 1940. "The whole of the warring nations are engaged, not only soldiers, but the entire population, men, women, and children. The fronts are everywhere. Trenches are dug in towns and streets. Every village is fortified. Every road is barred. The front line runs through the factories. Workmen are soldiers with different weapons but the same courage."

* * *

Between 1940 and 1942, the threat of invasion and the reality of aerial bombardment shocked the British nation. They urgently needed fighter planes. De Havilland was in the process of producing a small plane called the Mosquito, but to be fast, it had to be light, and they had not found a way to fix small plastic components securely to the wooden-lined walls of the plane. The vibrations of the Mosquito when in flight dislodged them. De Havilland sent out a call to all British plastics manufacturers asking for solutions.

Like his father, Walter was something of an inventor. And out of all the plastics firms in the whole country, it was he and Mica who solved the problem. His coworkers were delighted; they bought a barrel of beer, drank to his health, and carried him around the yard on their shoulders, cheering. Walter was told that he could claim payment for his crucial invention. But he never did. "I have no claim," he said. "It is the least I could have done for this country."

By the end of 1942, Walter had worked his way up from foreman to manager and then to director. That Christmas, Curlow arranged a party at the factory.

"Everyone is welcome," Walter said. "Staff, suppliers, customers, wives, husbands, boyfriends, girlfriends—everyone. There will be wine, beer, and whiskey, and we even have a dance band."

Walter didn't want me to wear an evening dress; he asked me to wear something simple. But I wanted to look my best, for several reasons.

"Can I wear the black crepe de chine with the yellow silk shawl?"

"Do you have to wear the shawl?"

"Yes."

"All right, wear your shawl."

The large room is smoky and smells of beer. The band is playing. Curlow greets me politely, avoiding my gaze. We are seated at his table with some of the other directors and managers. Seated opposite me, her elbows on the table, is a blue-eyed redhead in a lilac dress that clings to her body.

Walter's secretary.

Walter had never mentioned that he had a beautiful secretary. Or any kind of secretary.

We ate and drank and danced. I had been married twice; I had some experience in flirting. And I never trusted women. I knew that if you think she's after your husband, you need to watch *her*. At some point, she will give herself away. If she's stupid, she will be all over him, but if she's clever, she'll glance at him only occasionally, touch his hand accidentally, move her leg against his under the table, look into his eyes, and part her lips.

I felt her leg move, saw her look at my husband. So did Curlow. He frowned, looked at me, then smiled.

I didn't say anything to Walter. He would have denied it, and I had no proof. But there was no doubt that he had flirted with her. She was beautiful and bold, and Walter was vain.

A few days later, Walter asked me, "Do you remember my secretary?"

Do I? "Yes," I said. "Why?"

"Curlow sacked her the day after the party. Paid her two weeks' salary and told her to leave immediately. No one knows why."

8

The flat in Melina Court, St. John's Wood, is empty when we see it for the first time. Almost all the occupants of the block have left London for the safety of the countryside. The rooms are large and bright. There are glass doors opening onto a terrace. Trees are almost close enough to touch. I will plant red geraniums in terra-cotta pots all along the black railings. There is sunshine everywhere, crowding through the windows, through every door. Everything seems gilded. I want to sit on the wooden floor and sing.

Three weeks later, I am standing at the kitchen sink, washing china, glass, and cutlery and putting them away. The flat is No. 12; numbers divisible by three have always been lucky for me.

We find some good curtains. The carpets from Walter's flat in Vienna look wonderful. Our furniture, Mother's French clock, and our silver from Vienna make the place seem luxurious.

Things are looking up for us. Walter is doing very well at Mica, earning good money. Mr. Levy is delighted with my work at the Clarendon Hat Company and has increased my salary.

The train I took to Luton left at nine o'clock from St. Pancras. I was always late, arriving at the station just in time. The porters had got to know me and would keep the nearest carriage door open after the whistle had blown; they would shove me up into the carriage, roaring with laughter. They were always making bets that I would miss the train, but I never did.

One morning, my friends the porters have almost had to throw me bodily onto the train. Breathless, I walk along past full compartments until I reach one with a space. I sit down, look up, and find myself opposite a commuter I have come to think of as Edward G. Robinson. He is well dressed, elegant, and solid, and I have noticed him often.

That morning, as the train rattles out of St. Pancras, we begin to talk. His name is Meyer Woolfe. His father was a poor, Russian immigrant, a tailor who brought his children up to be hardworking, God-fearing, and honest. Meyer had married an East End milliner named Dora and started a wholesale business in the millinery trade. Eventually he went into retail, employing twenty-two girls to serve at the counters in his shop. He bought two factories, one in Whitechapel and one in Luton. Even with the war on, ladies were still wearing hats.

While his business had prospered, his life had been hard in other ways. His only son had been killed in a direct hit on the famous Café de Paris in Piccadilly in 1941. His young daughter was suffering from leukemia.

That evening, I sat in my favorite place, on the floor, with my head on Walter's knees. "Can you imagine how the man must suffer?"

After that, Mr. Woolfe and I often talked during the journey to Luton. Then one day, I was walking along the corridor when the door of a first-class compartment opened. Meyer beckoned me inside.

"But I have a second-class ticket," I protested.

"Be my guest." He laughed. "It's much more comfortable here."

There were six deep seats covered in thick, dark gray velvet. Clean white linen squares embroidered with the letters *LMS* were fixed to their backs. The carriage was empty.

"Now we can really talk," said Mr. Woolfe, taking the window seat opposite me.

I felt uncomfortable. I hardly knew him. Then he said, "I want you to come into business with me. The Reginald Hat Company needs someone like you."

"I *have* a job, thank you."

"With me, you'll have much more than a job. You'll have an important position in my company. Look, Mrs. Ehrlich, come to my factory this lunchtime, pick out some wooden blocks, choose some hoods. By tomorrow, I'll have them blocked. Take them home and make six model hats. I'd like to see your style."

A few days later, on the train, I said, "Your hats are ready, Mr. Woolfe."

"Could you bring them round to the house? We live in Finchley Road. I'd like my wife to see them. She's a partner in the business—although she hasn't done much since our son was killed."

"I am sorry, Mr. Woolfe, but I am not a *midinette*, arriving with boxes full of hats in Finchley Road. If you would like to see what I have done, please come to see me. I live in St. John's Wood."

He came, he saw, *I* conquered. He took my hats back to Finchley Road, and the next morning offered me a directorship and a salary of one thousand pounds a year.

"I'll think it over," I said.

A few days later, he asked for my decision.

"I am sorry, Mr. Woolfe, but I can't accept your generous offer. You see, working at the Clarendon Hat Company has made me realize that I want to start my own business again."

He didn't say a word, just looked out of the window until we reached Luton. I told Walter I had offended him.

I didn't see him the next day, nor the next. Then, the following Monday, he waited for me on the platform, took my arm, and led me to a first-class compartment. He offered me a partnership: thirty percent of the profits.

I told him again that I would think about it. This time, I felt embarrassed, but it was a difficult decision to have to make. I explained to Walter. "Look, Mrs. Woolfe is a partner, even if she has stopped working. Mr. Woolfe's brother holds no shares, but is a salesman and hopes to become a partner one day. This is a family business. One day, they might gang up on me. I am the outsider, and as the minority shareholder, I would have to do as they say. They might try to force me to sell, or drive me out by making me unhappy. I can't let myself get into a situation like that."

I told Mr. Woolfe, "I can only accept a fifty-fifty partnership with equal voting rights, and I know that is impossible. I don't have the money to buy half of the shares."

We had a meeting at Finchley Road: Walter, me, Mr. and Mrs. Woolfe, Mr. Woolfe's brother, and their lawyer. After that, there were more meetings, with more lawyers. It was decided that I would buy a one pound share that would hold fifty percent of the voting rights and thirty percent of the profits.

Six months later, Mr. Woolfe voluntarily raised my share of the profits to fifty percent, and we became joint managing directors.

"You know, Mrs. Ehrlich," he said, "if you had brought your hats round to Finchley Road, this would never have happened."

* * *

In 1944, De Havilland wrote to the Home Office recommending Walter's immediate naturalization. The application was backed up by a letter from Mica Products:

16 November 1944

Sir,

We are supporting Mr. Ehrlich's application for naturalization in the strongest possible way.

We have known Mr. Ehrlich for a period of four years, during which time he has been invaluable to this firm. He has worked wholeheartedly for the benefit of this nation in its war to defeat its enemies, and has played a very valuable part in at least one instance. In the production of Mosquito airplanes, a stage was reached where small components were causing worry to Messrs. de Havilland, and after endeavoring to get firms of much larger standing than ours to overcome this difficulty, it was left to our Mr. Ehrlich to discover a method whereby this component part could be used with safety in this extremely important aircraft. It was due entirely to Mr. Ehrlich's endeavors that this was brought about, and since, not only was he able to provide a method, but he followed this up by developing production of this component sufficiently to satisfy the very urgent need of the aircraft industry as a whole for this particular component.

Mr. Ehrlich is constantly introducing new ideas and new lines of thought in the production of our insulating components, and his abilities, we are sure, will stand this nation in good stead in the postwar years, where his inventive mind, together with his ability to put into practice his theories, will enable this firm to produce components of vital need in replacing the damaged electrical systems throughout the world, and he will be useful in our endeavors to expand our export trade, which HM Government have outlined already is going to be our lifeline in the future economic world.

Walter and I were among the first aliens to become naturalized British subjects. And because we thought "Ehrlich" was a difficult name for English tongues, and that it marked us out as foreigners, we changed our surname to "Ellis." I thought "Trudi Ellis" sounded right.

9

I hear him coming up in the lift. Walter looks tired. He sits down, looks past me. I go to get his slippers. When I come back, he is standing at the window, tears running down his face.

"Walter, what is it?"

"It's Curlow. He's dead."

I see Curlow standing in front of his bombed-out factory, arms outstretched, calling to his men, "Who is with me?" I am sitting opposite him in the Chinese restaurant as he bangs the table. He shouts, "Trudi, is it me or that damned letter?" We have never had a conversation since that row, but I know that he cared. And we had no family. We were refugees. Curlow's friendship was precious.

Churchill had warned us in a radio broadcast to expect new forms of attack from the enemy. In 1944, Hitler's new weapons, the V-1s and V-2s, terrorized us. In April 1945, the Allies entered Buchenwald and Belsen. What they found there was enough to destroy all faith in human nature. The newspapers described the British soldiers, sick with disgust and fury. My mother's sister and brother were still in Vienna when my parents left. We never found out what had happened to them. Mother and Father spent hours poring over the newspaper reports. My mother would ask me to translate the horrifying headlines and stories, and cry with her head buried in my father's shoulder.

On 7 May, the German Supreme Command surrendered unconditionally at Reims. The war in Europe was over. Eight May was declared VE Day. Walter and I followed the crowds along the streets of London. People wore red, white, and blue rosettes and paper crowns. We were at the very center of the rejoicing. At three o'clock, we heard Churchill broadcast to the nation from loudspeakers. We all sang "God Save the King."

The relief is overwhelming. Day and night, for years, we have lived in fear—of bombs, and of the Gestapo, its shadow stretching across the sea. Escaping our persecutors was like climbing a mountain, arriving at the top with bleeding hands. Now it is over.

Epilogue

(London, 1960)

Walter is told to sit upright in bed, to take hot baths. He is in pain across his chest and down his right arm.

"An inflammation of the nerves caused by an arthritic condition in the neck," says the neurologist.

I tell him that Walter has a slight temperature. He takes his blood pressure, arranges a blood test, and we are dismissed.

Walter can walk only very slowly. He has to go to bed. After three days, the hospital telephones to say that there is an infection in the blood. The doctor gives him a powerful penicillin injection.

I wake up during the night; Walter is sitting up.

"What's the matter, darling?" I ask.

"Oh, it's nothing. Don't worry. I . . ." He can't finish the sentence.

I turn the light on. He is unconscious. I telephone the doctor. I pour some brandy down his throat. He swallows.

"Walter, darling. Hold on. The doctor is on his way. Hold on, please!"

And no one can tell me that he didn't hear. He tried, he really did.

The doctor arrives in minutes, pajamas under his suit. He closes my husband's eyes. Inside me, I am still screaming.

"Human error," the doctors said.

I scatter roses over Walter's grave, a blanket of red roses. I pray. The sky is blue. The sun is shining. I feel his nearness. I remember Vienna. Walter stands on the glass roof. We sit in a nightclub by candlelight. We drink champagne in a restaurant.

WALTER ELLIS

12 JANUARY 1904–6 APRIL 1960

MOURNED BY HIS WIFE GERTRUD,

HIS RELATIVES, HIS FRIENDS

AND ALL WHO HAD THE PRIVILEGE

OF KNOWING HIM

Auf Wiedersehen, my love.

Some Girls, Some Hats and Hitler was first published in 1984. Trudi Kanter was born in Austria and moved across Europe as she tried to escape the Nazis. She managed to do so, finally settling in England with her husband, Walter. She died in 1992.

Virago Editor Ursula Doyle was the first person to rediscover Trudi Kanter's story. Here, in an article Doyle wrote for *Publishers Weekly,* she recalls the experience of finding and falling in love with Trudi's story.

"It was only three years ago, when I took a job at Virago . . . that I realized I had an opportunity to bring Trudi's story to a wider readership."

"Seduction and Serendipity"

A self-published memoir discovered on the shelf of a used bookstore gets a second life thirty years later

By URSULA DOYLE

In 1987, when I was an undergraduate, I was browsing in a bookshop in Cambridge, England, when a book (one copy, spine out, on a shelf in the back of the store) caught my eye: *Some Girls, Some Hats and Hitler* by Trudi Kanter. It was a self-published memoir, which, unusually for such a thing, had made its way into a mainstream bookshop—I can only imagine that the title had caught the buyer's attention, as it had mine.

I bought the book and read it, and it lodged in my mind: this true story of a young hat designer in Vienna in the 1930s. Trudi Kanter evoked that now-vanished world with incredible vividness; she had been a young, good-looking, independent woman who loved doing all the things that young women do: dancing, reading, visiting friends, flirting, falling in love. She saw no reason why her life would ever change. But of course it did—drastically.

I think almost anyone who has read an account of living in a country occupied by the Nazis tries to imagine finding themselves in that unimaginable situation. But before reading Kanter's book, most of the memoirs I had read about the experience of Europe's Jews before and during WWII came from places which to me, in 1987, felt far, far away—Poland, the U.S.S.R., Czechoslovakia—concealed behind the Iron Curtain, home to terrifying athletes and elderly waxwork leaders standing on balconies saluting never-ending parades of tanks. Vienna was different: it felt nearby, like Paris, or Rome. Reading Trudi's book brought the events of WWII much, much closer to home.

Trudi's life up until the arrival of the Germans in 1938 had been charmed. But she realized long before many of her contemporaries that the fact that her father was Jewish put her in danger. Trudi lied, bribed, coaxed, harassed, and bullied her way through every channel she could think of, official, unofficial, and criminal, to get herself and her fiancé,

Walter, out of the country. Once they were safe in London, she worked every avenue all over again to get her parents out.

In 1989, after graduating from university, I got a job at *Granta,* the literary magazine, as the editor's assistant. I stayed there for seven years and became the deputy editor; I then went to work at Picador, until 2008. It was only three years ago, when I took a job at Virago, which alongside a thriving frontlist, publishes books by women that have fallen out of print over the years, that I realized I had an opportunity to bring Trudi's story to a wider readership. The book had accompanied me throughout the slightly itinerant life many of us live during our twenties. It had been in and out of cardboard boxes and lent to friends; I had reread it several times. There it sat on my shelf with its 1980s cover, and occasionally I would think what a shame it was that Trudi's story wasn't more widely known. And in those intervening years, the world had changed; it was now possible to consult resources online to find out what had happened to her, and whether there were any surviving relatives who might hold copyright in her memoir.

I managed to establish that Trudi was born in 1905 and died in 1990; that she and Walter registered with the Jewish Refugee Council when they arrived in London in 1938; that there were census records of them at an address in St. John's Wood in the 1960s. But she was an only child who had no children, and Walter's family had all died in the Terezin concentration camp.

My colleagues fell in love with Trudi, whose personality

blazes through the pages of her book, and so in the end, we decided to go ahead and publish, including in our new edition an appeal for any further information regarding Trudi's estate (nobody has come forward yet). *Some Girls, Some Hats and Hitler* was selected by Waterstones for its book club, which ensured front-of-store display in its branches. Trudi was born a writer. Her descriptions of her life in prewar Vienna—the wonderful food, the ever-changing fashions, the glorious music, the lush gardens, the romantic cafés—are almost unbearably vivid: unbearable because one thinks of her sitting down in London in her late seventies to remember it all.

And Trudi either did not know or, I prefer to think, did not care how she came across at various points: haughty, treacherous, disloyal, or mendacious, why did it matter? Her memoir is a story of love and hatred, of civilization and barbarism, of home and exile, and above all, of the heroism of a completely ordinary, extraordinary woman. And it's back on the shelves to enchant readers the way it enchanted me.

A Scribner Reading Group Guide

This reading group guide for *Some Girls, Some Hats and Hitler: A True Love Story* includes an introduction, discussion questions, and ideas for enhancing your book club. The suggested questions are intended to help your reading group find new and interesting angles and topics for your discussion. We hope that these ideas will enrich your conversation and increase your enjoyment of the book.

Introduction

In London, in 1984, Trudi Kanter's remarkable memoir was published by N. Spearman. Largely unread, it went out of print until it was rediscovered by a British editor in 2011, and now, for the first time, it is available to readers everywhere. In 1938 Trudi Miller, stunningly beautiful, chic, and charismatic, was a hat designer for the best-dressed women in Vienna. She frequented cafés. She had suitors. She flew to Paris to see the latest fashions. And she fell deeply in love with Walter Ehrlich, a charming and romantic businessman. But as Hitler's tanks roll into Austria, the world this young Jewish couple knows and loves collapses, leaving them desperate to find a way to survive.

Some Girls, Some Hats and Hitler is an enchanting true story that moves from Vienna to Prague to blitzed London, as Trudi seeks safety for her and Walter amid the horror engulfing Europe. In prose that cuts straight to the bone, Trudi Kanter has shared her indelible story. *Some Girls, Some Hats and Hitler* is destined to become a World War II classic.

Topics & Questions for Discussion

1. The subtitle of this memoir is *A True Love Story*. How much of Kanter's tale is a love story, and how much a war story? How did the experience of war bring Trudi and Walter closer together?

2. When Trudi tried to convince Walter to flee Vienna in 1938, he responded, "You know that you always put your head down and charge at the wall, whereas I need to think carefully before I make a decision" (p. 36). How did the differences in Trudi and Walter's decision-making affect their chances of survival?

3. Describing the anti-Semitic mobs in 1938 Vienna, Trudi wrote, "This is the truth about what happened, but I feel some reluctance to write it down" (p. 45). Why did Trudi

hesitate to describe the realities of Nazi Vienna? Do you think she portrayed the people of Vienna fairly? Why or why not?

4. Consider the role that jealousy played in Trudi and Walter's relationship. When did Trudi worry about losing Walter to other women? Did her fears seem justified? Why or why not?

5. Discuss Trudi's relationship with her ex-husband, Pepi. How did they manage to remain close after the end of their marriage? In what ways did Trudi have trouble letting Pepi go?

6. Consider the gender roles in Trudi and Walter's relationship. How did Walter handle Trudi's success as a designer? How did Trudi deal with Walter's slow career start in London? In what ways were Trudi and Walter ahead of their time, in terms of gender and the workplace?

7. During their first weeks in London, Trudi observed in frustration, "No one will let us forget that we are foreigners! . . . It's a dirty word!" (p. 162). Discuss how Trudi and Walter were treated in London. What kinds of discrimination did they face?

8. Trudi wrote, "Now that I am married to Walter, I have come to realize that there can't be red roses every day.

A good marriage means having someone to talk to at night, someone you can fight with and fuss over. Someone you can trust" (p. 205). Discuss Trudi and Walter's transition from daily roses to everyday trust. What did Trudi gain and lose when she married Walter?

9. When Trudi fought off Mr. Curlow's romantic advances, she discovered, "Even in my smart clothes, with my sophisticated maquillage, my two marriages and all my recent experiences, I am still an immature girl" (p. 235). Did you think of Trudi as an "immature girl" or an experienced woman when you read her memoir? Explain your answer.

10. Discuss how the war affected Trudi's relationship with her parents.

11. Consider the ups and downs of Trudi's career as a hat designer. How did she manage to advance in her career, even as a new immigrant to London? Which of her designs sounded the most innovative?

12. "This was the time when a feather and a sequin was a hat" (p. 25). Discuss the changing hat fashions during the years Trudi described in her memoir. Which fashions sounded the most alluring? Which could you picture women wearing today?

13. When Mr. Curlow's factory was bombed, he said to his workers, "We'll build it all up again, everything as it was.... Brick by brick, floors and ceilings, water and electricity. All of it! Who is with me?" (p. 238). How did Walter react to Mr. Curlow's determination to rebuild? How did Mr. Curlow's statement capture the spirit of wartime England?

14. The end of the memoir briefly describes the end of Walter's life. What was particularly tragic about Walter's death in 1960? Do you think this memoir of love and war was difficult for Trudi to write? Why or why not?

15. *Some Girls, Some Hats and Hitler* was originally published in England in 1984 but went largely unread. Why do you think today's readers might be especially interested in Trudi's story? How are her struggles and adventures relevant to readers today?

Enhance Your Book Club

1. Ask members of your book club to wear their favorite hats to your meeting! From retro cloches to modern sun hats, compare your favorite pieces of stylish and practical headwear.

2. Browse an online exhibit of wartime Vienna—including photographs, personal histories, artifacts and maps—at

the United States Holocaust Memorial Museum's website: http://www.ushmm.org/wlc/en/article.php?ModuleId= 10005452.

3. Read all about the history of women's hat fashions, from the eighteenth century through the twentieth century: http://vintagefashionguild.org/fashion-history/the-history-of-womens-hats/.

4. Treat your book club to a taste of Vienna! Bake a batch of decadent Sachertorte, a traditional café dessert, and serve it at your book club meeting. Find a recipe here: http://www.epicurious.com/recipes/food/views/Sacher torte-231043.

5. "Walter and I used to play a game," Trudi writes—they would quiz each other on the contents of Walter's long-lost home in Vienna (p. 52). Pair off in your book club and ask your partner to remember details of her first childhood home. What color were the bedroom curtains; how many lamps were in the living room; what did the kitchen cabinets look like?

See more at simonandschuster.com.